I'm so grateful to have Billy Terrell in my life via ——— who was abandoned when I was four days old and taken to Mang Lang Orphanage, which Billy and other soldiers in his company helped establish near the village of Tuy Hoa in 1966. Fortunately, I was adopted at the age of two by Austrian parents who reside in Australia. I have no idea where I would be today if it weren't for Billy and other US soldiers who graciously cared for and comforted the children of Vietnam. If I had one dream come true, it would be to meet him and thank him. —**Joy Wimmer**

The story of Billy Terrell is the story of how one can find fulfillment in life by following his or her passion. It reminds me of a chapter from my book, *You Only Rock Once*, where you rise above all obstacles by following your heart. —**Jerry Blavat, The Geator with the Heator, Author of *You Only Rock Once***

Billy Terrell's career spans a lifetime as a musician, songwriter, music producer, and comedian. This book takes you on a ride through those years and beyond. It's an excellent read through the comedic mind of one of the funniest men I've ever known. —**Jerry Gross, The Dovells**

A great read. Billy Terrell remarkably evolved from a bullied kid to a war hero, hit songwriter, and record producer. —**Peggy Santiglia Ricker, The Angels**

Billy Terrell is a singer/songwriter, musician, producer, author, and very special friend. Through many years and many miles, we traveled together. I have always felt that his story needed to be told, and *The Other Side of Rock and War* takes you through the good and the bad and out the other side. It's quite a remarkable journey. I am proud that Billy has written this book and proud of his well-deserved success. —**Gary Criss, Recording Artist**

I will never forget the first time I met Billy Terrell and Ray Dahrouge. The look in Billy's eyes was saying, *You've got to listen to our songs*. He was so sure of himself that he reminded me of myself when I started out. Two young white guys telling me they had the songs I was looking for, and they were right! Their songs were as black as coal. Great R&B songs, great hit songs. Billy's book is just like his songs: GREAT, GREAT, GREAT! —**George Kerr, Record Producer**

THE OTHER SIDE OF
Rock AND **WAR**

To ETHan,

Keepin' THE music ALive!

Bobby Dear

THE OTHER SIDE OF
Rock AND **WAR**

ONE MAN'S BATTLE
TO SAVE HIS LIFE, HIS CAREER, HIS COUNTRY,
AND THE ORPHANS HE LEFT BEHIND

BILLY TERRELL

with
Rich Podolsky

Foreword by **FRANKIE AVALON**

PRESENTED BY THE NATIONAL FOUNDATION *of* PATRIOTISM

Published by:
National Foundation of Patriotism
Buford, Georgia
In association with Brass Parrot Media Partner, LLC

ISBN: 978-1-7323427-0-5
eISBN: 978-1-7323427-1-2

Book Design: GKS Creative
Project Management: The Cadence Group

Library of Congress information is on file with the publisher.

Table of Contents

NATIONAL FOUNDATION of PATRIOTISM

The National Foundation of Patriotism
is proud to present
The Other Side of Rock and War

This book is an individual account of an era that belonged to all of us. A book every Vietnam veteran could be proud of, and every citizen should be aware of.

The National Foundation of Patriotism is dedicated to supporting, promoting and preserving this piece of American history because of its surprisingly positive message and its powerful historic relevance.

About the National Foundation of Patriotism

The Foundation is an independent, non-profit educational organization dedicated to increasing awareness about the history of patriotism in America.

Our Goal
To inspire, educate, and empower everyday citizens to respect our country, learn about our history, care about our citizens and preserve our freedom by honoring our U.S. Constitution and our American flag.

Your partners in patriotism,

Nicholas D. Snider
Founder / Chairman

Pat Stansbury
Executive Director

P.O. Box 1726, Buford, GA 30515   404.875.0691
www.foundationofpatriotism.org

Foreword
by Frankie Avalon

BILLY, BILLY, BILLY . . . TALENT, TALENT, TALENT . . .
FRIEND, FRIEND, FRIENDSHIP!

Back in 1976 music and song styles were changing through the years. Like many singers at that time, I was in limbo as a recording artist trying to deal with those changing styles until Billy Terrell entered my musical world. He came to me with an idea of rerecording the biggest hit I've had ever had, "Venus," with an idea of rerecording the song in a style that was emerging around the world called disco.

He sat at the piano and played for me what he thought it would sound like in the style of disco. My answer was, "No way! 'Venus' is a classic record that should not be touched." The record label was reluctant, as well, as the song publishing rights were not easily available. But Billy was positive it was right and convinced us to allow him to have the musicians to play his arrangement as the last song on the session, and if we didn't like it, we didn't have to use it. Needless to say, I loved it.

To my amazement, when the record came out, the disco version of "Venus" became number one on the Billboard charts once again and furthered my career. It led to four television specials and ultimately an opportunity to appear in the huge hit film version of *Grease* as Teen Angel. It also afforded me a new recording career making several more albums.

During the recording of the *Venus* album in Philadelphia, a disturbing incident occurred with Billy. We were to meet in the lobby of our hotel to go to the session when I was told he had been taken to the hospital with a very high fever. When I went to see him in the hospital, he was suffering from a blood disorder that was initially suspected to be caused by recurring malaria that nearly took his life ten years earlier in Vietnam.

You, the reader, will have the opportunity to read the story of a man, his music, his life, and dedication to his country. *The Other Side of Rock and War* is an emotional roller coaster cover to cover.

—Frankie Avalon

Author's Note

IT'S SEPTEMBER 20, 1988. THE ROOM IS BUZZING WITH anticipation. From offstage the audience hears: "Catch A Rising Star now proudly presents the comedy talents of Billy Terrell."

Warm applause runs through the smoke-filled room. A funny-looking, balding forty-three-year-old man with dark horned-rimmed glasses bounces out to center stage.

"My name is Billy Terrell, ladies and gentlemen. I'm from Newark, New Jersey. I'm the only guy that got to Vietnam and felt it was an improvement!"

"My father couldn't hold down a job. We got evicted fifty-eight times. One day I asked, 'Ma, can my friend Harold sleep over?' She said, 'Billy, we're not even sleeping over!'"

"We were dirt poor. All us kids slept in one bed. When it got cold my mother threw another brother on."

My stand-up comedy routine got big laughs, but it was all true. You might even say sad but true. Fortunately, there was a happy ending.

Introduction
The Torsiellos: From Naples to Newark

I WAS BORN ON NOVEMBER 14, 1944, IN NEWARK, New Jersey, at Columbus Hospital. Forty-two years earlier my great-grandfather, Antonio Torsiello, brought the family here from Campania, near Salerno, in the southern part of Italy. He took my great-grandmother and all eight children to the Port of Naples, where on November 5, 1902, they left on the *Palatia*, a ship that accommodated sixty first-class passengers and two thousand in third class. Thirteen days later, they arrived at Ellis Island.

The ship, which was built just eight years earlier, eventually wound up as part of the Russian Navy. After some sleuthing, I located and printed out the captain's manifest from the Ellis Island website. The captain wrote in the manifest my grandfather's name, Pasquale Torsiello—who was just twelve years old—and the address in Newark, New Jersey, where the family was headed.

They settled in Newark, and the story goes that my great-grandfather didn't like it here and he wanted to go back to Italy. But my father told me that my great-grandmother was having none of it.

"If you want to go back to Italy," she told him, "go ahead, but I want the children in America. I want them to be in this country."

So, he packed up and just went back and no one ever heard from him again. But there are two versions, two possible realities. Some people say that he never went back, and he lived upstairs in an attic somewhere. There's another story floating around that some people think he went back to Italy, got married again, and had another eight kids. So I don't know what story works out, but, yes, the family came and stayed here.

My great-grandmother, she was like a rock, from what they tell me, and very close to my father. My grandmother, Mary Fabio, my father's mother, was born on 11th Street in Newark in 1893. Her father was from Northern Italy and her mother was French. She married my grandfather Pasquale in June 1913. She taught my grandfather how to speak English and was the rock in the family all her life. My grandmother was a workhorse. My grandfather was in construction.

I remember my grandmother going to church every day, as she lived right across from St. Francis Church on 8th Street. I watched that church being built in Newark in 1951. My grandmother used to take me with her when she had tea with Louise Pesci (grandmother of the future actor Joe) in the late '40s. They were lifelong friends, having been born next door to each other on 11th Street in the mid 1890s. She passed away at age seventy-nine in 1972.

My grandfather was a great bricklayer and a great guy. I miss him today. He worked very hard and eventually started his own construction business with a lot of help from Grandma. By the mid '20s he was building houses and renting them out in Newark. He was a very honest man who took extreme pride in his work. Before he went in business for himself, he would walk off jobs if the bosses told him to work fast and not worry about perfection. He wore a tie every day he went to work even though it wasn't that kind of work. He took pride in everything he did and was very respected his entire life.

He built up such a nice business by the late '20s on 11th Street in Newark, he built and owned most of the homes on one side of the street and rented them out. He was doing great. When the Depression hit, he lost everything—their home, the business, and all the income properties. He was such a wonderful guy; when the people couldn't afford to pay the rent and the bank couldn't give him any more money to continue the business, instead of doing what a lot of people would do, throw the people out, he wouldn't do it. Not only did he keep them in there, my father told me many times my grandfather would have my grandmother give him big plates of macaroni and loaves of Italian bread to take to the families. So that's the kind of guy he was.

Then, shortly after losing everything, he had a terrible nervous breakdown. My grandmother had to work on the sewing machine all day, sewing stuff, taking in laundry and doing all she could to keep things moving along. My grandmother was so well respected in the neighborhood that when my grandfather's older brother Sabato shot a guy in the head who was giving my grandfather a hard time, the local don put the word on the street to let it go. That's Mary Fabio's family!

My mother's father, Walter Gimbel, was born in NYC on West 41st Street in the same apartment house as James Cagney, the actor. His family was from Germany. He met my grandmother, Lillian MacNeil (she was Scottish and Irish), in Belleville, New Jersey, and I believe they were also married in 1913. They ultimately had eight children: Walter, Lillian, Charles, Viola, Eleanor (my mother), Robert, Donald, and Doris. He built a house on Courtland Avenue in Belleville where the family lived until he lost the home during the Depression because he couldn't pay seventy dollars in back taxes. Grandpa Walter worked as a painter and was a great sketch artist and musician. His work is still on the walls of schools and government buildings in Newark and Belleville. Incredible talent.

Grandpa Walter was an interesting character. He played every musical instrument. Really! He even built his own instruments. He made his own violin. He made a xylophone. He used to play the piano in the silent movies. He used to be in the theater; while the picture was going, he'd add the music. He was also a marvelous artist with sketches and paintings. Then when the Depression hit, he lost his home and it threw him into the bottle. He had eight kids and lost his home because he couldn't pay seventy freaking dollars in taxes. My mother told me he was so demoralized that he went so poorly downhill and wound up in shelters. My uncles would have to go find him. Then, ultimately, when I was six months old, he disappeared and they never heard from him again.

My grandfather Walter also had a nephew, William Gimbel, who had his own set of troubles and became an arch criminal. On January 19, 1930, he robbed the A&P supermarket in Belleville; as he attempted to get away, he fired three shots, killing one person and wounding two others. They didn't mess around in New Jersey in those days because on December 29, 1930, he went to the electric chair. He was only twenty-one years old.

My grandmother (my mother's mother) was a very quiet lady. I didn't know her very well. She used to sit by the window, drink wine, and just smoke cigarettes and always pulled the cigarette with her fingers down and with the cigarette pointing toward the floor. I remember even as a little boy asking my mother a few times about my grandmother's habit.

"Why are Grandma's fingers so brown and dark?"

"Well, it's from the cigarettes," she told me. Obviously, my grandmother never really recovered from my grandfather disappearing. She passed away in 1959. I believe she was sixty-nine years old. It was a rough existence. The promise of America, which was so great when they arrived, was wiped away with the pain that the Depression brought on.

ONE

I Felt My Father's Pain

MY FATHER WAS NAMED VITO WILLIAM TORSIELLO, after his Uncle Vito, and was born March 13, 1914. Uncle Vito died at the tender age of nineteen for no good reason at all. He was shot in a bar during an argument in a card game, and no, he wasn't holding aces and eights.

My father was about 5'5" and around 150 pounds, I would guess. He was very stocky and muscular, having been in construction. He had brown hair, olive complexion, and brown eyes. He smoked Camel cigarettes constantly but really wasn't much of a drinker. He would have a little burgundy wine on occasion or a brandy when he went out to sing at various places.

He was actually a Big Band singer in the '30s, up until World War II. He also worked as a singer with a pianist. Then he had his own band, Bill Tarrell and His Orchestra, and played New York clubs and sang on NBC radio. Then World War II came along and it broke up the band. He was drafted and he went to the army, finished basic training, and then, he was medically discharged because he had a fractured skull as a kid. He was complaining of headaches, so they tested him.

His whole unit was moving out to Guadalcanal and they kept testing him, testing him, and they couldn't find anything wrong with him. So they sent back to Newark for his medical records. What they found was that while he had helped a guy on a coal truck when he was thirteen, they had an accident and my father went through the windshield and lost a lot of blood and fractured his skull. So, with that in his records, they couldn't disprove that he was having problems so, they let him out. When he came back, he worked in a defense plant up in Belleville, Wallace and Tiernan, which specialized in water chlorination. And that's where he met my mother.

But my father was still really intrigued with music and he once again began singing in clubs like The Blue Moon and the Flagship in and around Newark. Afterward, when he married my mother, she just was very insecure and hated the music—hated him performing.

Then I came along, then my brother Richie and my sister Mary came along, and there were five of us. He was demoralized, but at that point, he went into construction and he worked hard but mentally, he never left the stage. In the late '40s, early '50s, with the help of my grandfather, he'd built up a nice business after the war when the economy picked up.

We lived on 6th Street near Franklin Avenue for quite a while, and then my father's business really took hold. Interestingly, the gentleman—I don't know his first name, this fellow Einhorn—loved my father's work. He was a big developer. So, he gave my father a very lucrative contract to build housing units. It was enough money to hire twenty-two employees. He also gave my father a property in Belleville that became our brand new home months later. My father got a $10,000 construction loan from the bank, and he and my grandfather built the whole house. They brought in an electrician and a plumber, but my father and grandfather did the rest of the construction. They worked together.

Things looked up when he got the big contract. We had a new home, two cars, and a truck, and we were one of the only families in the neighborhood with a television. I would have never thought, at that point, we would soon be penniless and forced to move twenty-one times in the next decade.

———————

Unfortunately, my mother had a lot of difficulties. She was about 5'1", very thin with brown hair and eyes. She had a light complexion, as she was a mixture of German/Irish/Scottish. She smoked Winston and Viceroy cigarettes like a chimney and drank a lot of beer. Schaefer was her favorite. She would demand my father go out almost every night and buy her one or two quarts of Schaefer beer. Sometimes she would wait until the stores were about to close and scream at my father to go get her beer. He never resisted it, though, even knowing she had already had too much and that it would be a long night. I never understood the hold she had over him, because he knew two quarts of Schaefer would turn her into the devil. It was very sad.

When my mother was sixteen, she was running around with a married man and my grandmother was afraid she'd get pregnant. To stop her, my grandmother had her sent away to a state facility for a time. I don't think my father ever knew. We only recently found out about it because our cousin Gladys wrote it in her memoirs prior to her passing. Here's a record of it from the 1940 Census:

> Eleanor Gimble
> 1940 Census
> Ward 14, Trenton, Trenton City,
> Mercer, New Jersey, United States
> Female Age 16
> Single White Inmate
> Last Residence: Belleville, New Jersey

When he was doing okay in the building business, my father was offered a chance to go to Las Vegas, which was booming then, to build hotels. This is when they started in the early '50s and some interesting characters that he knew through his life in Newark, New Jersey, had contacts out there and invested in some of those hotel-casinos. My father had the opportunity to move there and heaven knows what we would have been like, but there's no way my mother would go.

That was another big, demoralizing step for my father. He had to get out of Belleville because there were a lot of problems with my mother's family, so he moved. He gave up the construction business and we moved to Belmar, New Jersey. It was a terrible existence for many years after that.

My mother was physically abusive at times. She never hit me, but my other brothers would get hit with a pancake turner. My sister Mary got it too. I don't remember my baby sister, Patty, getting hit, but I was much older than her and not around as much. My father never raised a hand to any of us. The most difficult reality was that he was there but not there. He was not affectionate at all and a horrible provider after walking away from his business. Most of what I refer to as abuse was the hardship of going to bed cold and hungry many, many times.

Our clothes were very few and not in great shape. My brothers and I had two or three pairs of pants and a few shirts. My sister Mary at one point only had one blouse and one skirt to wear to school. She washed them every night and ironed them every morning.

My mother wasn't a good cook at all. She really didn't pay much attention to taking care of the house either. It seemed like she did just enough because it was expected of her. Her food was awful. My father, on the other hand, was great on Sundays when we could afford it. He learned the greatest recipe for gravy sauce from my grandmother. When he would cook on Sunday, it was a treat: macaroni, tomato sauce, and huge meatballs with raisins in them.

My mother had a drinking problem. It caused a lot of problems for me growing up. It's interesting—it's sad, really—how both sides of the family, both sets of grandparents, went so far downhill with the Depression.

Prior to marrying my mother, my father performed with a lot of very cool people. He told me he was in his glory. He worked clubs like the Normandy, the Miami Club—these are all North Jersey clubs—and the Nineteenth Hole, back when the nightclub business was the nightclub business. People dressed up, they went out. He worked with artists like Lou Monte, who was famous. He also was the house singer at the Miami Club when Jackie Gleason was the MC.

He told me some great stories about Gleason, because Gleason was not only a big drinker, but he just ate and ate. He wasn't a great comedian, but he had a lot of moxie on stage. My father told me that at the Miami Club, people heckled Gleason a lot. Then, sometimes, Gleason would invite them out in the alley and he would win these fights. So this one night, there was a guy in a party, and the guy was drunk. He was really on Gleason. Gleason was fed up with it and he invited him into the alley, not knowing it was Two Ton Tony Galento, the only fighter up to that time who had knocked down Joe Louis. My father said Gleason obviously didn't know what he was doing. My father recognized the guy, but before he could go to the manager and say, "You better tell Jackie to bag that," he didn't get out the door and Galento hit him with one shot and it took a half-hour to wake him up. Yes, Gleason was a wild guy, always broke, great pool player, always bumming cigarettes.

Then, my father became very friendly with Buddy Rich, who was a great drummer who played with Sinatra, played in his own band, a lot of bands, rough guy, tough guy, but my father became very friendly with him. My father played the Roxy and Buddy played the Roxy and my father used to hang out with him. My father was younger, so he used to go get Buddy's car and go get his clothes from the cleaners and stuff. He liked Buddy Rich. He met Frank Sinatra but only once. Sinatra was back playing the small clubs after leaving the Tommy Dorsey Orchestra. As a matter of fact, Sinatra's car broke down once and my father and a few other guys pushed the car, but he didn't really know Sinatra all that well. Most of those clubs were owned by gangsters. Gyp DeCarlo, a loan shark who worked for the Genovese crime family, was one. My father did a lot of work for Gyp DeCarlo at the Flagship in Union, New Jersey, and he also knew quite a few other colorful characters. Our family, our immediate family, were cool and law abiding. We had other characters in the family that, back in the '20s and '30s, were not so cool.

My father really wasn't a musician. He just sang, and then he led the band. He told me he was intrigued when he first heard Bing Crosby on the radio. He just really liked Bing Crosby and Russ Columbo. He told me that it was Russ Columbo who really inspired him to pursue a career in music. He explained how it all began. He was at a party when he was in his early twenties where they had live music. He walked up to a microphone and started singing into it. He really loved it; he really found it fascinating to hear himself on a speaker. That's what jumpstarted the whole thing for him. Then, he went out and started working the small clubs, and he built it up to where he ultimately put his own orchestra together. I still have his banner, "Bill Tarrell and His Orchestra," that survived.

It was T-A-R-R-E-L-L. He put an "A" in it. A friend of his, Phil Biasi, said, "You need a show business name." He said, "Let me see," and he said, "Tarrell." I think there was a guy named Farrell back then, so he said, "Why don't you just make it Tarrell?" It's a T, and it stuck. Then, when I got in the business in 1963, which we'll get to later, I shortened it. My first publicity was T-A-R-E-L. I dropped an "R" and dropped an "L."

Then when I got my first manager, he said, "That sounds like a Big Band singer."

I said, "Well, it was." He wanted to make it Torrell and I said, "Well, if you're going to go that far, then, let's put the R and L back and make it Terrell, like Tammi Terrell," and that was that.

When my father first met my mother, she was working on an assembly line. My father was in charge of the manufacturing demonstration of water purification. He told me that some people from the military—officers from the service—would come in and he would demonstrate the water purification systems. He'd take rainwater or something and put it in there and it ran through the thing, and then he'd take it and he'd drink it. So, he would demonstrate for them that this is a safe thing, and then the army would—or whatever service—would order a certain number of these purification units.

That was his job. Then, he met my mother. She was only nineteen and he was twenty-eight, I think. He turned twenty-nine in 1943. I think he met her probably in early '43. They went out and he didn't seem all that interested. Then she came to the house one day, and my grandmother said, "Willie, there's a young girl here to see you." One thing led to another.

My dad and I sat up quite a few nights talking back in the '50s and '60s. He liked talking to me, I guess, because I was fascinated by his show business stories and how it all unfolded. He said when World War II broke out, most of his friends and key musicians were drafted. He had no band—the guys weren't around. He couldn't put the band he wanted back together. He figured he was twenty-nine and my mother was desperate to get out of her situation, which we didn't realize until later, and he asked my mother if she wanted to get married. She said yes. She turned twenty on November 19, 1943. They were married February 10, 1944. My father turned thirty the following month, on March 31. It must've been a busy wedding night because I was born exactly nine months and four days later.

This is the earliest known photo of me with my parents in early 1945 in Newark.

My mother was still twenty on the 14th of November and she turned twenty-one on the 19th. So, there was that age gap. There was also a cultural gap. My father lived in a real peaceful home, even though they didn't have very much money—they had it before the Depression, though. He had a great dad, great mother, an Italian mother. That was family, church, and serenity. Then, he winds up in this situation where there was a lot of alcohol in the family that he married into. My mother had a lot of emotional trouble. She married too young. They had a really, rough time but they were together right until the end. I mean, it would've never lasted today, in a million years, but they stuck it out.

So, he said to me that he wasn't getting any younger and the war was raging. It didn't look like he was going to be able to make a good run back at music, so he got married, thinking he could do both—that he would work and then do his music on weekends—but my mother just hated it. She wouldn't have anything to do with it. He had kids coming and rather than throw the towel in—and thank God that he didn't—he stuck it out. I felt bad for him, but at the end of the day, it worked out better for us that he did stick it out, even though it was a terrible existence all through the 1950s. It was volatile then, too, because my parents' relationship really deteriorated quickly. It was a very uncomfortable situation. They argued and fought all the time. There was a lot of infidelity in my mother's side of the family, which was painful. Infidelity played a terrible role in all of it.

I didn't realize it growing up, but I've realized it for quite a few years now—*that I felt my father's pain.* I didn't understand it and I didn't understand at the time what I was feeling, but now I realize I really felt his pain. I always mentally stuck with him however I could. My brother Robbie had a very volatile relationship with my father and my brother Richie, too, at times. But me, I always had a soft spot for my father, because I felt his pain. I knew he wasn't happy, and that bothered me.

My mother's problems were deep rooted in an abusive environment growing up. Her oldest brother, Walter, sexually abused his sisters, and that had to take a toll on my mother. I remember when I was about four years old seeing my Uncle Walter kiss my mother passionately. I never forgot that or understood it for the longest time. We weren't aware how bad it was until she passed away in her sleep at age sixty-five on August 15, 1989. Relatives were never close with us because of how far apart we lived. After she died, they began telling us of the horror my mother and her sisters went through growing up in that house.

There's no doubt in my mind that my mother got married so young to get away from home, not because of being in love with my father. It is now obvious she carried great guilt from her sexually abusive childhood all her life. She had a heart of gold but when she drank, the dark side took over and it was bad. She started running with other men when I was about four years old. I witnessed the infidelity for several years and it was very painful.

My father challenged her several times but stayed with us regardless. I think that's why I always had a soft spot for him even though he didn't take responsibility, as he should have, as a father and family man. My mother and Aunt Viola, her closest sister in age, often ran with men together. Aunt Vi, as we called her, was a nice lady, but she, too, had an unhappy marriage and drank too much. She was also one of Walter's victims. I believe the number one reason my father moved us out of Belleville and to the shore was to get my mother away from Aunt Vi and their running around with men together.

My parents had five children. I'm the oldest, and then my brother Richie was born in '46. My sister Mary was born in '47. Then in June of '53, my brother Robbie was born, who passed away a few years ago. Then July 23rd of 1960, my kid sister, Patty, was born, and she was the last one.

We moved to Belmar, New Jersey, in 1952. They moved down in the spring and I stayed with my grandmother to finish the school year in Newark, and then when the school year was over, I went down. They were bouncing around. They lived in a small apartment in Long Branch. Then, when I moved down, we moved into the Princess Hotel in Asbury Park on the top floor. We had one room with the bathroom down the hall. We all lived in that hotel room. My father still had some money from the house he sold. He obviously just went through the money like crazy and that started our downfall. And my mother was drinking and still unfaithful.

I remember the Princess Hotel being a very big hotel. That year, in 1952, there were three of us kids. I was seven going on eight. My brother probably was six, going to be seven. My sister, Mary, she was four, because she would have been five on September 26. I still get the chills when I think that my mother would go out in the hallway where we lived and there was a door onto the roof and she would sit there and smoke her Winstons. The three of us would be playing ball out on that flat roof. I think back on that and I wonder, *What was she thinking?* I remember chasing the ball right to the edge of the roof, and I was seven years old. We could've sailed right over it. It freaks me out to think about that. So, we were there for the summer, and then we moved. At that point the madness really took hold, because we moved like, oh, god, tons of times. So, we moved over a furniture store from there. It was a ratty—really a ratty—place with some crazy people around. That was in the fall of '52.

We went from there, and then we started moving, mainly because my father, he would work, but then he'd be out of work. Then he'd do a job, and then he'd be looking for another job. He did independent jobs, instead of just going and saying—and I discussed it with him at the end of his life—instead of saying, "Hey, all right, I'm a good bricklayer, I'm a good construction guy. I better get in with a good company, because I have three kids. Okay, I lost everything, but now I got to step up to the plate," but he didn't. It was like he would work, and then he wouldn't work.

So, after the apartment over the furniture store, we moved to Bradley Beach on McCabe Avenue, and that started the cycle of moving every six months throughout the '50s. We lived on McCabe Avenue until the spring of '53. Shortly after moving to 17th Avenue in Belmar, my brother Robbie was born. Then we bounced around. We bounced back and forth all over Belmar. For the following seven years, when it got close to summertime, we would have to move into the west part of town, away from the beach, because the rents were less out there. You couldn't rent near the ocean, but then come the end of September, we would take a very cheap place at the beach because they would love to have you there just to watch the place. We were constantly evicted because my father would always be behind on the rent and they would throw us out.

My father was always broke, and we were always living poor. A tragedy was that they didn't buy us toothbrushes or teach us hygiene, and my teeth were very, very bad. It made my life miserable. We didn't have a lot of food, so I was underweight. I think back to that and it drives me crazy. But somehow, they always had money for cigarettes and my mother's beer. In the mid '50s, both my parents would smoke first thing in the morning. The kitchen was a cancer den. I often would take my bowl of cereal and sit out on the back stoop and eat, even if it was snowing out.

Then, at the end of the summer in '56, the guys who owned the Aloha Hotel on 4th Avenue near the beach said to my father, "Look, Bill, we're going to Florida for the winter. Why don't you move your family in the house next to the hotel, free? You can stay in there until next May. In this way, all you pay are the utilities and you'll be able to catch up, because you won't have rent. It's good for us because you can keep an eye on the hotel. If there's something wrong, a pipe breaks or something, you're there. You can take care of it."

Well, as unbelievable as that seems, now that we were in this place with no rent, my father had his worst year because the less responsibility he had, the less he did. By Christmas, we had no utilities. None. He put four cement blocks in the living room and a kerosene stove there. It got so cold that my father had to use sheetrock to close off the stairwell to the second floor where all the bedrooms were. My sister and brother and I, we slept in one bed in a room on the first floor, and my parents slept in a back room of the house with Robbie in his crib because we couldn't afford to heat the whole house.

Even though we went to bed cold and hungry, it didn't stop me from making light of our situation. We did get a few small Christmas gifts sent to us from relatives. But they were ridiculous. My sister, Mary, got a cookie baking kit. She made these awful cookies that were as hard as hockey pucks. My mother ate one and within an hour she was on her knees with her head in the toilet. I was making so many jokes she was screaming and throwing up at the same time. I was on fire. One after another I kept the jokes coming.

"How would Santa Claus even know we are here?" I asked, laughing. "We have no lights, no chimney, it's ice cold, and if he ate the cookies, he'd die." And then I said, "I was hoping we *would* get coal in our stockings, at least we could warm up."

As bad as it was that Christmas, we found time to laugh. The following spring, we were evicted again. Still with no utilities. Incredible!

This was the '50s. Most of America was thriving after World War II, but not my family. We had a Depression-like existence.

TWO

We Had Nothing—Not Even a Toothbrush

THE WINTER OF 1957 WAS ONE OF THE WORST WINTERS I remember. I had to walk a mile and a half to school and all I had was a thin jacket. There was a lake, Silver Lake, and it was frozen solid. I used to walk across it because it would cut the time out and especially because I was freezing. I had no hat. I had this very thin coat, a zipper jacket. It took me a long time to make my peace with that, because, of course, back then there wasn't the DYFS or Division of Youth and Family Services. It took me a long time to make my peace with the school, because I don't know why they wouldn't call my parents in and say, "What's up with this?"

Then, my teeth were terrible. We used to have these exams by the school dentist. This is Belmar Grammar School in New Jersey. I went in there and I was always so embarrassed to have my teeth looked at, because they were so bad. They were awful. I remember thinking back to those days and thinking, *How could that dentist do that? How could he be so rude?* And he was rude to me. How could he look at a young kid like that and not get involved somehow? At least call the parents in and say,

"Hey, there are clinics, dummy, why aren't you sending this boy to one?" It took me a long time for me to make my peace with it and to come to terms with it.

Shortly after moving to the Shore, when I lived on McCabe Avenue in Bradley, I went to the Bradley Beach Grammar School for short time. I entered late, but I finished that year, even though we moved over to Belmar. So, I entered Belmar Grammar School in September '53. I was there until I graduated in 1959, even though we kept moving. Then we moved to 11th Avenue near Main Street. Then to Maplewood Road. Then, we moved to West Belmar, to 17th. From there, we moved to 21st Street, which was really a hilarious story. We started bouncing through town like every four or five months; we would be thrown out and we'd go to another place.

I've been doing stand-up comedy for quite a few years, for over thirty years. I talk a lot about the poor days: *"We moved so many times, I used to call home after school for directions."*

It's a true story, because in October of '55, I didn't know we were behind the rent again. It was about ten o'clock at night and my father woke me up and said, "Get up—we're moving." I held up the shade and it was dark.

"What do you mean, 'We're moving'?"

"We got to get out of here," he said. The sheriff was there with the landlord. Today, they'd never be able to do it. We never had a phone, so my father had to walk to the corner—I guess a gas station—and called a friend of his that had a truck and then he called another friend of his that was a cab driver. We put what we could in the truck and, in the middle of the night, we moved into the next town over where the cab driver had us sleeping on the floor in sleeping bags. So, the next morning, I got up and the cab driver drove me to school. Before I got out of the car, I said, "Well, how do I get home?" I think he gave me a dime, might've been a nickel. The phones were cheap.

He gave me his card and he gave me the coin and he said, "After school, call me and I'll give you directions how to get home." You can't make something like that up.

That was very difficult, but the most painful Christmas wasn't even '56. It was funny, really. I had to make jokes about it, because it was so ridiculous. I laughed through it, even being cold and hungry; I still look back with some fond memories, because it was so hilarious, but '55 was very painful.

There was a diner for many years in Belmar called Pat's Diner. The owner was a marvelous, marvelous man. In 1955, he got together with the school and he hired a bus and he had the school gather all the underprivileged kids, most of whom were blacks and there were some whites. They sent a bus and we all met at the school on Christmas Eve. They took us to Pat's Diner and he had a wonderful meal for us and we all got gifts. They took us in the bus again. We went to the Rivoli Theater and, I'll never forget, they treated us to the movie *Calamity Jane* with Doris Day.

As beautiful as it was, the painful thing was that the more fortunate kids in the north side of Belmar, a lot of the affluent ones, were mean. A lot of their fathers were doctors and lawyers and those kids could be mean. It was so painful, because it was such a lovely experience for us, because most of us didn't have food and it was such a nice thing. Until some of the rich kids showed up on their bicycles. They were making fun of us through the window. A couple of those idiots went as far as to spit at the window and that cut deep for many years. It was just horrible, such a nice event and somebody went that far out of their way to do something nice for us and the underprivileged colored kids, I mean, God! We referred to them as colored kids back then. It really wasn't a problem. We played with them. We lived on the same economic level. They had their boards on the windows and no heat; we had boards on our windows and no heat. So, we had real camaraderie there. I didn't only feel sorry for myself, I just felt sorry for the racial remarks and spitting on the window.

I had one friend, a marvelous friend, Joe Buxbaum, who lived on the next street, a Jewish fellow. My brother Richie and I, we played ball with him all the time. We just loved baseball and Joe was my friend. My brother was popular. My brother was a good-looking kid. His teeth held up. He was in the same environment, but his teeth held up and the girls all loved Richie. Nobody seemed to like me. I was buried under all this negativity. To escape it what we did was, we played games. We didn't have anything. We just improvised.

I remember in '57 we used to get these wooden fruit baskets from the back of the A&P supermarket on F Street. We used to find them, that were damaged, and we'd cut the bottom off. We had a basketball that never held all the air. You'd have to slam it on the ground. We nailed that wooden basket to the telephone pole. I can tell you that those games—we played into the night, were some of the greatest games you can imagine.

Many nights we played until it got too dark. Often my sister Mary, then nine years old, would join in so we could have two teams. Baseball from the spring all the way up to the winter was the greatest. We had these old, rickety gloves that I think were given to us or we might have found them in the trash, and we played the greatest games, and Joe was our buddy. Baseball was like a religion to us. They were sacred times that took us far away from any of the difficulties at home. In the summer we would play early in the morning until noon, go back out until around 4:30, eat supper, and go back out until dark. Sometimes we even played in the rain. Richie was a great player. Joe and I were average players, but it was all in fun.

In the summer in Belmar, people would leave all their garbage on the beach at the end of the day. The township cleaned up everything—

cigarettes, paper bags, food, and empty soda bottles. Each night they had plows and would come out and clean up the beaches. We used to go out and pick up as many bottles as we could before the plows came. We took them back to the beachfront stores and got two cents for each returned bottle. Most evenings we would each wind up with between twenty-five and thirty-five cents. Richie and Joe would spend most of their shares at the penny arcade and maybe buy a soda or candy. I spent most of mine on Topps baseball cards. I loved them. At one point, I had both the 1956 and 1957 complete series in two cigar boxes. Who would have known that in 1979 those two sets along with our signed NY Yankee baseball would have fetched over a million dollars? Well, maybe not quite a million.

Joe stuck by me and he was a guy that was tormented as well. He lived with his mother and his grandmother and his sister. His sister was kind of retarded and nobody liked Joe either. It was sad. His dad was in World War II, came home, and died. He was in the navy. He came home—he was home about six months—and he passed. Joe was raised in this home with all girls and ladies. For some reason, the other kids didn't like Joe, either, so Joe and I stuck together. I still think of him as my first friend.

He had a trust fund and they were doing okay. I remember, many times, Joe would treat me to something. We'd go to the Sugar Bowl, down by the Rivoli Theater, after school, and he would buy ice cream sodas. We played ball and that's how we kept ourselves occupied. It was a survival thing and the baseball was our salvation.

That summer, we used to go down to the 5th Avenue Beach, beyond the Pavilion. We used to go over there and throw the ball. That wasn't a busy beach, behind the Pavilion, so some of the professional ballplayers from the Yankees and whoever were playing the Yankees would go down during the day. We got to meet Jimmy Piersall from the Red Sox. We got to hang out with Bill "Moose" Skowron and Andy Carey from the

Yankees. They would even play catch with us. One day, Bill and Andy came down and Bill said, "Hey, I got a present for you guys," and he took out two baseballs, both signed, by the entire 1957 Yankees. He gave one to me and my brother and he gave one to Joe.

A few months later we went to play over near the river on the one lot where we played sandlot ball. My brother fouled our old ball that we played with all summer right in the water. Now, we have no money for another ball and we went for, I think, two or three days. It was toward the end of the summer. We couldn't play baseball and we were going out of our mind and I said to my brother, "Do you know what?" I went up and I got the baseball, the Yankees ball. We played the rest of the year with the ball signed by the whole Yankees team, a signed baseball. That's how much we loved baseball. We wore the signatures right off the ball. We had that ball—even in 1960, we had it. That's crazy stuff.

So, everyday life might have been painful and about to get worse, but Joe and Richie and I found a way to put that aside, at least for a wonderful summer playing baseball on 5th Avenue Beach.

THREE

High School Was a Nightmare

WE DIDN'T HAVE A CAR AND WE DIDN'T REALLY GET A telephone until, I think, it was actually into the '60s. Most of our relatives were up near Newark and East Orange, but my grandparents were in North Caldwell. When we had a car that would run, we would go up to visit them. All through the '50s, however, I don't ever remember us visiting our aunts or uncles. Other than my grandfather, I think we had one visit from one aunt and uncle. From what I understand after talking to my godmother before she passed away, the family was just so annoyed with my father for our situation.

Well, I mean, rest his soul; he was irresponsible. He's the provider. My mother, she didn't work until years later. We did maintain a good relationship with my grandparents. I just didn't see them a lot.

Toward the end of my seventh grade school year at Belmar Grammar in 1958, my teeth were at their worst at that point. My four front teeth were rotted and brittle. I used to be able to move them back and forth with my tongue. One day at my desk one of my front teeth broke off and skipped along the desk to the floor. It was a nightmare. Many of the bullies laughed and made horrible jokes tormenting me until the summer break. They used to call me "Gums" and would leave jawbreakers candy on my desk and snicker behind my back. I don't remember any of the girls ever making remarks or giving me rude looks. But the boys were brutal.

My father couldn't avoid it any longer. He took me to a dentist and the dentist took out the four front teeth because they were just shot. I was sick as a baby and they gave me a lot of tetracycline in the hospital. My first teeth came in black. They weren't white teeth; they were black teeth! Then, they fell out, and then, my other teeth came in white, but they were very brittle. So, I had what was left of my four front teeth taken out and I had to go through the eighth grade, graduate, and go through the whole first year of high school at Manasquan High School in a living hell. You learn a lot of lessons about human behavior when you're in that situation. In Manasquan, they were extremely mean to me.

Two of the daily classes were outside of our main building quite far from our homeroom. This created a golden opportunity for the bullies to rough me up and get away with it. To get to agriculture class, we had to cross a stream on a wooden bridge. Several times a week, I would be thrown in the water. The thing that hurt was not one teacher ever questioned why my clothes were wet when I entered their classrooms after agriculture.

I remember Fridays were dress-up day and the school colors were blue and gray. I only had two pairs of pants and they were black and green. When I mentioned it in my comedy act, I would say, *"If I wanted to go to school on dress-up day, I either had to go to Ireland or North Vietnam."* It might have been funny in the clubs and on paper but not in real time, believe me.

Manasquan was near Brielle and some affluent areas. We had our poor guys too. I mean, my black friends from Belmar that went to Manasquan, they were with me. I had nothing, and they had less. Whenever I had a little milk, I used to share, or if I were lucky enough to have a sandwich, I would share a little food with them, because they looked out for me.

They obviously related and resented how I was treated over only having two worn out pairs of pants. Black and green. The problem was, with our school colors being blue and gray, that made my life even more miserable. Not only did they make fun of me for not having teeth, but I was also getting smacked around because I wasn't "with the school." So, I stopped going to school on Fridays and eventually I was called into the office and sent to see the guidance counselor.

"How old are you?" he asked.

"I'm fifteen," I said.

"You're not supposed to be working," he said.

I said, "I'm not working."

"You're not working? You're not working?" he said with astonishment.

"I'm not working. I wouldn't lie to you—for what?"

"Well, then," he asked, "what are you doing on Fridays? You're not coming to school on Fridays."

"I'm not learning anything on Fridays. It's dress-up day and I only have two pairs of pants. I have black and green and, when I come to school without these blue and gray school colors, I'm getting smacked around. I'm getting ridiculed. I'm getting thrown in the creek. This is so miserable with nothing to wear," I told him, and he just stared at me, I guess for ten seconds. It seemed like a lot longer.

"All right," he finally said. "I'll take this into consideration, but you're going to have to come to school. I'm going to have to talk to the homeroom teacher, and we're going to have to put an end to this."

"Well, whatever you can do," I said, "but I hope you can understand that this is a miserable existence."

By the time the Christmas and the New Year break came along, I had taken so much abuse from the more privileged white kids, the colored boys started sticking up for me. I can see now that we shared each other's pain.

The last day of school before we broke for the holidays, it was snowing like crazy. Waist-high snow and coming down so hard you couldn't see more than a few feet in front of you. We had science class far from the main building. One of the bullies started in on me hard, believing he would get away with it with no witnesses. Wrong! As soon as class let out, the snow was coming down harder, which made it even more difficult to see. It was a perfect opportunity for two of my colored friends to do their magic. One bully took such a savage beating that he wasn't back in school until February. There were no witnesses.

I was called in again by the guidance counselor and grilled for over an hour. He was convinced I had something to do with it. I didn't give him anything, but I remember saying to myself he must have a reason for coming to me, so why didn't anyone get involved before this had to happen? Obviously, the faculty just looked the other way. The poor kids (white and colored) were treated equally—like dirt! I was reminded of that reality several times in Vietnam. After that savage beating, nobody would dare even look at me. They wouldn't bother me. They would walk on the other side of the street. It was not a proud moment, but you've got to survive. The black boys felt bad for me because I was thin and picked on constantly. Thank God for them. They stuck up for me. Those are not such great memories.

Then, after school got out for the summer, we moved again. This time to Shark River Hills. I started my second year in Neptune High School and it was worse. I couldn't afford their colors, either, which were red and black. What really made it worst for me, Manasquan High and Neptune High were major rivals. Every time they played basketball, there would be a fight. Football, there'd be a fight. They hated each other. The first day I had to show up for gym class, I had no choice but to wear the only gym clothes I had, blue and gray. The Manasquan colors. I couldn't afford anything else. I came running out on the floor in my Manasquan gym clothes and darn near got killed. Bullies cornered me in the locker room, threw me, my street clothes, and all my books in the shower, and turned the water on full blast. I got kicked and left there soaking wet. I stumbled down to the principal's office and walked in drenched.

He asked, "What happened to you?"

"I don't think I'm going to make it here," I told him. And that was the end of high school for me.

I turned sixteen that November. We were doing very poorly at that point. My sister, Pat, was just born, so we had a little baby there and my other two brothers and sister. My father came to me and said, "You got to leave school."

"What do you mean?" I said.

"You got to quit school. You got to go to work."

"Well, where am I going to work, and if I quit school, what am I going to do?"

"Well, you got to do it," he told me.

I realized at that point I was going nowhere. I didn't really want to leave school, but my father spared me from making the decision. He basically forced me to quit school. I wasn't learning anything anyway, and I was getting beat up a lot. There were many times when I was in Vietnam, I used to say to myself, "If I make it out of here, I'm going to get even with those idiots." Of course, I didn't do it.

So, I gave in and quit. I walked a five-mile radius for months trying to get a job. I knocked on every single business—real estate offices, luncheonettes, and the movie theater. No one would hire me. After all, who would hire a high school dropout with four front teeth missing?

Beautiful Aunt Laura, circa 1940.

FOUR

Aunt Laura to the Rescue

NOW, WE'RE GETTING INTO THE WINTER OF 1961. IT was a bad winter and I'm walking in waist-high snow. To bring money home, I would shovel snow, rake leaves, and clean attics. I was scrubbing floors too. I would just go around and ask people if they needed any dirty work done, just to pick up three dollars, five dollars. On my way home, I would stop at the Cracker Barrel food store, buy milk and groceries, and bring them home.

After a few months of looking for a job, I came home one day, and I could tell my father was not happy with me. "You know what?" he said, referring to a nearby donut shop. "Do you know that they just hired somebody over there?"

"They didn't hire me," I told him. "I was there two or three times and they wouldn't hire me."

"Well, God damn it," he said. "They hired him."

"Dad, they turned me down more than once. I've been there. How many times am I going to go knock on a door and they slam it in my face?"

The truth was they didn't want to hire someone who had their four front teeth missing. My father was very, very hard on me but I've made my peace with it. Looking back, part of it had to be how frustrated he was himself.

Somehow, I got through the summer of '61. We moved back to Bradley Beach, on Monmouth Avenue, but not for long, because we got thrown out of that place. At the end of that summer I was working at a bingo hall, sweeping up and helping set up the tables and chairs and whatever else needed to be done.

At that point, I was turning seventeen, and I just looked at my future and I thought, *I've got to go to school. If he kills me, he kills me, but I got to go to school. He made me quit to get a job and bring some money home, but no one would hire me.*

"Look," I said to my father. "I'm going to go. In September, I'm going over to Asbury Park High School and I'm going to see if they'll take me. I want to go back to school."

I started my second year over again at Asbury Park High, but it was bad. I was getting roughed up daily. The bullying was worse than the other two high schools put together. There were very mean people up there and, of course, with no teeth it was even worse. It was awful. I don't think I made it through two months. After about a month and a half, I went down to the principal's office.

"I'm out of here, out. I can't do it," I said to him. "It's worse now than it was at the other two places. I'm just going to leave."

I was deeply embarrassed about having to quit school. I was always embarrassed about the way I looked. I mean, I was a smart kid. I know that now. It took me a very long time to realize that I'm a smart person, but when you're in that environment, it's hard to view yourself as being smart. You're fighting social issues and economic issues. So I really didn't learn much. I really wasn't learning anything of any consequence. I wasn't doing terrible on the tests, but I wasn't breaking any walls down and I was certainly not getting any breaks. I mean, it was all on me. Plus, I had gone to bed cold and hungry so many times.

My Aunt Laura picked up on it. She came down and talked to me about my situation. Aunt Laura lived with my grandparents, was never married, worked at the Prudential Insurance in Newark, New Jersey, as a receptionist. She was a marvelous person who truly cared. I know she rests in peace.

"Bill," she said, "I talked to Grandma and Grandpa, and I'm going to bring you up to Newark and you're going to live with us. It's going to take time, but I'm going to have a dentist fix these teeth."

She took me up and it took a few months. They had to take out most of my teeth. They left six on the top and six on the bottom. Back then they put in these clip-on dentures. They would clip onto the other teeth.

My Aunt Laura was the only one that seemed to care about what happened to me. I remember meeting her for lunch in Newark a few weeks after coming home from Vietnam in June 1967 and expressing my anxiety about not having an education and wondering what the future would hold for me going forward. God bless her soul! She gave me the greatest advice I still live by today: "Bill, you're a smart man! Everything you need to learn is free at the public library. The key is to learn to use the language properly and you will have all the power you need."

A few days after getting my new front teeth was when I got the music bug. I was looking in the mirror at my smile and thought, *Wow, that's wild.* My grandmother's radio was on, The Tokens' hit song *The Lion Sleeps Tonight* was playing, and I remember singing along with it. The song was infectious.

I continued to live with my grandparents a few more months. It was a great time because I ate well and my grandfather would take me for walks. I had turned seventeen and my grandfather was still taking me for walks, but I loved my grandfather. He was a wonderful guy. We used to walk down to Branch Brook Park every day.

On the way down there, God bless him, he used to stop at this bar and he'd have a shot of Four Roses Whiskey and a beer and I'd have a Coke with a cherry in it. Then, we'd go to the park and we'd walk all around, and then, on the way home, he'd stop at the bar at the other side of the street for a shot of Four Roses and a beer. We'd get home and his face would be all red and my grandmother would give him a tough time, but he was a great, great man. I miss him every day. It sounds ridiculous, but most days, I always think of something that triggers him.

I did not try to enroll in school in Newark. That was the end of it. Howard Johnson's was opening in February '62 on the Boardwalk in Asbury Park. They were just opening. I went and applied for a job and I was hired! I was hired as a dishwasher and busboy. I remember how elated I was. Somebody gave me a job! I was accepted! I remember that whole feeling. I said to myself, "Wow, that is something else. Somebody finally stepped up to the plate." I was one of the first people hired in that first wave at HoJo's. They hired a lot of people, but I was one of the first group that they brought on board. It was fifteen dollars a week or some dumb thing. To me, it was more than fifteen a week; it was that I was accepted.

I remember the first day. I was working back in the kitchen. Again, I was at home working with poor black boys and some Puerto Rican boys. I was back in my element. I mean, I could relate and I was just so happy to have somebody hire me. I worked very hard and I remember a waitress coming in. I'll never forget her. Her name was Nora. These Greek people owned the place and they were very mean. She came in the kitchen the first day it opened, during the lunch rush, and said to Terry, the owner, "Terry, whatever you do, don't lose him—that kid works. He works harder than anybody I've ever seen."

I wanted to make an impression. I wanted to work hard. I had a job. So, now, it comes time to eat.

"Billy," the owner said in this Greek accent. "Billy, time to eat, time to sit down and eat. What would you like to eat?" He handed me a menu and I looked at the menu.

"Wow, yes, I would really love some of this roast beef."

"You can't have roast beef," he said. "Dishwashers can't have roast beef. You can have a club sandwich or a halibut steak."

I understand today that you can't give the employees the most expensive thing on the menu; economically, it just doesn't work. What offended me was the way he said it. I mean, if I can only have a club sandwich or halibut steak, for crying out loud, why don't you just tell me, "Employees can get one of two choices?" To make matters worse, I said, "Okay, well, no problem, I'll try the halibut. Halibut sounds pretty good." He gave me the plate and I started walking out toward the counter.

"Billy, where are you going?" he asked.

"Well, I'm going to go eat."

"No, you can't go near the customers. You have to sit in the back."

He made me feel like I was in the back of the bus. In the back of the kitchen, near the back door, it was very dark. They had a dirty piece of plywood held up by two milk cartons with no tablecloth, and the seats were soda-bottle boxes—the wooden boxes—back then. I remember taking the plate in the back and sitting at the table—well, what should have been a table—and I remember it clear as a bell. I said to myself, "I don't know what I'm going to do with my life, but I'm going to figure this out and, somehow, I'm going to get to a point where I'm never going to be in a position where somebody can tell me that I'm not worth a piece of roast beef after giving a hard day's work."

Lo and behold, that's how my music career kicked in!

It was July of '62 in Asbury Park, which is still one of the great Jersey Shore towns. In the '60s it was booming. That summer you could smell the popcorn and cotton candy as people walked by on the Boardwalk. They came for the sun and the beach and the great club scene at night.

I was working at Howard Johnson's, located right next door to Convention Hall, and now that I finally had my four front teeth replaced, I felt good about myself for the first time in my life. I had a smile and I had job. It didn't take much.

Convention Hall was where all the concerts, boxing matches, wrestling matches, and all the rock and roll shows were held in Asbury Park. The show next door at that time was an all Cameo-Parkway show. Cameo-Parkway was a Philadelphia-based record company with artists like Chubby Checker, Dee Dee Sharp, The Orlons, and The Dovells—music that I loved, which I'd bought back when I had the pennies to buy their records. Back then records were only thirty-nine cents or something. I took all the money I made that summer and I put it into the house. I didn't keep money for myself. I had to bring every dime home, because, at that time, we were five kids, a mother, and a father in a one-bedroom apartment. My mother and father slept in what was the dining room with Patty next to them in a crib. My sister Mary slept on a couch in the living room and my brothers and I slept in the same bed in the bedroom.

So, I'm busing tables at Howard Johnson's and in walked The Dovells in their suits, all dressed alike, and I loved The Dovells. I loved the "Bristol Stomp" and those records. They sat in the station that I was busing for the waitress. I was just totally taken by that. I met the guys and I got their autographs. For a long time, I kept the placemats The Dovells used! They autographed those for me.

That's what I'm going to do, I said to myself. *I have to get involved with the music that I love.* I didn't know how, but I knew I'd find a way. So, I scrounged up a little money here and there. I put most of the money in the house or we'd have starved. I couldn't do that to my sisters and brothers.

In the summers of '62 and '63, Asbury Park was amazing. It was a fascinating time. We had clubs like the Living Room, which became the Student Prince where Bruce Springsteen worked. We had the African Room; we had the Albion Hotel and the Rainbow Room. We had Mrs. Jay's, which is now The Stone Pony. We had the Candy Cane Lounge at the Lincoln Hotel. We had the Pillow Talk on Cookman Avenue, the Chez Charles, which was the gay place there at that time. In the black section, we had Big Bill's and we had the Orchid Lounge. Entertainment ruled the day, and I made up my mind to be part of it.

I sang a little and I worked up a bit of a stand-up routine. I started working the strip as an MC on weekends for $7.50 a night. I remember one night, I was at the Candy Cane Lounge and I was the MC. I was eighteen years old and the MC opening for Johnny Maestro and the Crests, who had "Sixteen Candles," before he changed it to Johnny Maestro and the Brooklyn Bridge.

In town at the Convention Hall was a big wrestling match. The Graham Brothers were twins, Eddie and Gerry Graham. They weren't really twins but just said they were. They were very famous wrestlers. They were like mountains. They were big, big guys. They were staying at the hotel, so when they came back from the match, they'd come in Candy Cane lounge. I'm up there opening for Johnny Maestro, playing a few songs, doing a few jokes, and they start heckling me. So, I said a dumb thing like, "I could take 'em both." As a joke, the Graham Brothers stood up. We meet on the dance floor and we start wrestling. Next to them I looked like a toothpick. They're making believe I'm beating them both and the audience was hysterical. They were going crazy. I said, "Ladies and gentlemen, the Graham Brothers," and they're applauding.

"Okay, well, we're going to move this show along right now," I continued, "and one of my favorite acts of all time, ladies and gentlemen, a nice hand for Johnny Maestro and the Crests."

The Crests come out and I'm walking backstage and Johnny's about to come out and he grabs my arm and he says, "How the hell am I going to follow that?"

"You're the headliner," I said. "Good luck."

I learned a lot about how to walk on and off stage there. I was still at Howard Johnson's in '63, and one of the waitresses was dating the bell captain at the Empress Motel. The Empress Motel was the crème de la crème back then in Asbury Park. It was like the Rat Pack days. So the bell captain used to come in for coffee in his uniform to see Jane down in Howard Johnson's. We would talk and, one day, he called me over.

"Do you know what?" he said matter-of-factly. "I've been watching you. You're a very hard worker. How would you like it if I talked to the Empress and see if I can get you over there for some good money? I think you'll do great."

I was thrilled but all I could say was, "I'd really appreciate that."

So, he got me a job in the restaurant while we were still living in Bradley Beach in that one-bedroom place. What I did was, I volunteered for every shift. I would go in the morning and bus tables for breakfast and I would do room service for lunch. I'd go home for a few hours in the afternoon and then come back and I'd bus tables for dinner. I would hang out and then do room service until midnight. So, I was working about fourteen hours a day and my only day off was the first Monday of every month. I was bringing every nickel home and I was supporting the entire family! The only thing I bought myself was a forty-dollar Kay guitar and Mel Bay chord book. I taught myself how to play it and then I started doing little gigs on the strip. That was during the heyday of Asbury Park, with a hotel and nightclub on every corner.

Where I made most of my money was on Sundays. The top two suites on the south end of the building, which had the best view of the ocean, were right on Ocean Avenue. They would rent those two suites out, open the doors going in and there'd be three big round tables in each one. Gangsters and high rollers would come in from all over the country and they would play highstakes poker games up there. I mean tens of thousands of dollars, in 1963. I was the kid they trusted to bring sandwiches and drinks when they wanted room service. The bell captain that got me the job said, "They like you. They don't want anybody else going up there; so, you're going to bring the food. You're the only guy." And I would make more money that day than I made all week.

The hotel did fine because they did big events. They did corporate events. The nightclub was sensational. Back then entertainment was king. And, when the Empress was open, the rock groups that played Convention Hall would all go there. They wouldn't go to the Lincoln and the Albion anymore. They would stay at the Empress, because it was *the* place, the modern place. I was working my butt off and the band used to like to get me up to sing on Saturday nights, because by Saturday night, I was really dragging. I finished my last room service and I'd go down in the lounge.

I went in there one night and the band got me up and I was singing "Pennies from Heaven" and "Walking My Baby Back Home." Then I was going into some jokes about room service because we had a lot of weddings, a lot of bridal suites. I finished that set that night and the waitress came over to me.

"Hey, Billy," she said. "That table would like to say hello to you." At the table was the show that was in town. It was Clay Cole, who was the Dick Clark of New York. He was the host. He had a big television show in New York, *The Clay Cole Show*. And at his table were Gene Pitney, Clyde McPhatter, and Paul & Paula. They all had hit records at the time—and there was also a guy named Brad Connelly who was Clay's roommate at the Bryant Hotel in New York. So, I walked over to their table.

"You're a really talented kid," Clay said.

"Oh, thanks," I said. "I enjoy it."

"If you want to come to New York and meet with us, we'd like to introduce you to a manager that I think would really get into what you're doing."

By then I had blossomed. I had the hair and I had that Frankie Avalon look. Suddenly, I was a good-looking kid.

"Well," I said, then paused because I couldn't believe what I was hearing.

"When's your next day off?"

"I only get one day off a month." He gave me the number of the Bryant Hotel.

"Well, the next day you can, let us know a little ahead of time and come up."

I went up to the Bryant Hotel, and I met with Clay and Brad. They had a guy named Vic Catala there who was managing the Bill Black Combo. He was also managing Barry Sadler, who later on would have the big hit "The Ballad of the Green Berets" but at that time, he hadn't hit yet. He had that hit while I was in the war. Then there I was, and on July 16th of '63, I signed my first management contract with Vic Catala.

We did some demos and walked around. He took me to the New York Institute of Photography and I posed for the students and I got free head shots. That's what really jumpstarted it. Shortly after I received copies of my head shot, I was able to get my very first write-up in *Spotlight Magazine* in Asbury: a blurb with the photo announcing that I signed a management contract with Vic Catala, who was also managing The Bill Black Combo (Elvis Presley's backup band on his earliest recordings and live performances). Thank God that Aunt Laura saved a copy.

But we couldn't get a record label interested. I went in and did some demos. They were the first demos I ever recorded, which was a thrill, but we weren't getting anywhere. The big problem was that I didn't have any original songs. So, I started writing my own songs.

Vic got busy and he couldn't move me, and we ended the relationship amicably. But I had had a taste and caught the bug. I started pounding the pavement as a songwriter and I was working the small clubs to get experience. I was trying to do the teen idol thing. And for the first time in my life, I felt great.

I stopped for a minute, took it all in—where I'd been and where I was going. Today I look back and I'm reminded of a lyric from the great Cole Porter song:

Is it for all time or simply a lark?
Is it Granada I see or only Asbury Park?

I was about to find out.

I blossomed at eighteen, and this was my Frankie Avalon look

FIVE

The Jersey Beatles

NEAR THE END OF '63, THE CRAZIEST THING HAPPENED. I met Larry Oxley, who was going around singing and playing guitar as Ricky Leigh. His two favorite performers were Brenda Lee and Ricky Nelson. So, he called himself Ricky Leigh and he spelled it L-E-I-G-H, crazy guy that he was. He would go around to record hops and sing his record, "Why Do Little Girls Hurt Little Boys," which was released on the Savoy label that summer. I was also going around to the record hops and would sing "Traveling Man," originally by Ricky Nelson. It was my first demo. I had an acetate disk with the vocal version and just the music track to sing live with it. I got to sing at those hops with guys like Jimmy Charles, who had the hit song "A Million to One." Many up-and-coming acts played the record hops to promote their records.

So I became friendly with Larry, or Ricky Leigh, and then we started writing a little bit by the end of '63. Going into '64, after severing ties with Vic Catala, Larry and I would go around to bars and pizza places and ask if we could sing for tips. Not all agreed, so we also took to singing on the boardwalk in Asbury Park to attract attention. We were approached by some people from New York who liked our harmony and invited us to a meeting in the city, but it didn't work out. We were trying anything to move our act forward. We weren't really getting anywhere, and then The Beatles come out.

Knucklehead that I was, I came up with a brainstorm. I said, "Wait a minute. Suppose we let our hair grow a little bit and we call ourselves 'The Jersey Beatles.'" Oh, it was so stupid, but we caught on because the fad was catching on and everything was Beatles. So, we started going to these clubs as The Jersey Beatles and many put us on as a novelty act. Before you knew it, the people are digging it, and the kids started digging it. Then the newspapers picked up on it. The Lyric movie theater in Asbury hired us to play before showing the film *The Greatest Show on Earth.* Can you imagine—The Jersey Beatles? They billed the show *The Greatest Show on Earth–The Jersey Beatles.* We're up there and we weren't that good, but you never heard a minute of music, because all those kids would do is scream.

At that point, we felt we were ready to record together as a duo. We went to New York and auditioned for the guys at O.D.O. Recording on West 54th Street. They took a chance and recorded us on a song we wrote called "Beatle Troubles." A gimmicky song about how boyfriends were so jealous of how their girls were hung up on The Beatles. We recorded it in late '64 with Wally Zober producing, who wrote a few of Fabian's hit songs in the late '50s. Wally also helped us polish up the song, but it was so dumb we couldn't give it away. No label would put it out.

So we went back to the Jersey Shore where we were still local favorites and soon wound up getting booked on a big rock and roll show at Convention Hall in Asbury Park. The show was loaded with unknown acts that were promoted by a big New York agency. All the acts were up and coming and pretty good, including the backup band for the show. Someone in the marketing department at Convention Hall suggested putting us on the show. He said, "Hey, you know what?

We ought to get those Jersey cuckoo birds. They draw. The kids love those guys."

So, we go on around the middle of the show. There must have been four or five thousand kids in the audience. We walk out on stage with one acoustic guitar, which Larry played, one microphone, and without the backup band. It didn't mean a thing.

The other bands were looking and saying, "There are thousands of people out there. What are they thinking?" They found out real fast. The screams were deafening all through the set. We played three songs. We played "All My Loving," "She Loves You," and then one of our own songs, "Who's the Boy?" I think it was a dumb, stupid song, but the audience went wild anyway.

As we walked off, I heard one of the members of another group say, "What was that? They're terrible."

I went over to him and I said, "They never heard a note."

It was a similar experience the real Beatles had at Shea Stadium in 1964. I spent some time with George Harrison and Ravi Shankar in London in '98. I had him on the floor telling him about The Jersey Beatles. He went crazy. He related to our experience very well. Of all the people I met in the business along the way, George Harrison was the most gracious. Great guy! I did get to meet with Paul McCartney, also very gracious, in 2004 at his office in New York City to play him a recording of "No More Lonely Nights" that I produced with Bobbie Eakes. He loved the version and kept it on the front page of his website for an entire year. What an honor.

It was great meeting and hanging with George Harrison and
Ravi Shankar in London in 1998.

Another Jersey Beatles story happened at the Ocean Ice Palace in Brick Township, New Jersey, in the fall of '64. Every Tuesday night, the ice rink used to have a rock and roll show. Danny Stiles, the Kat Man, who was on WNJR in Newark, used to put a show on and whoever had the number one record that week in New York on WMCA was usually the headliner. Danny also featured local acts. They always wanted The Jersey Beatles because the kids absolutely loved us. They used to tear our clothes off. We opened shows for The Dixie Cups when "The Chapel of Love" (1964) was number one, and The Platters, and comedian Soupy Sales when he had the number one record with "The Mouse."

So, after a month or so of Tuesday evening blowouts, the Ocean Ice Palace called me and said, "Look, we've got a road show coming to town, and we're going to have a family night on a Wednesday, and we were thinking that maybe putting you guys on the bill would entertain the kids because it's a folk music show."

"Well, I like it," I told them. "I'd like to make the money, but when were you thinking of putting us on?"

They said, "Well, you guys will go up first and do a short show to warm up the crowd."

I said, "Yes, but, if you put us on first, it's over. I mean, you see what happens here."

They said, "Well, look, we're paying a lot of money. This is a national touring show."

A few weeks later we show up to perform. They had a young black comedian, a folk band called the Hootin' Annies, and the headliner was Beverly Wright, a talented singer. The management insisted we go on first, and I said, "Okay, but I warned you."

So, the Jersey Cuckoo Birds go on first and the place went crazy, screaming. Girls are coming up on the stage. They had me by the foot. I'm trying to play and they're dragging me. Finally, they called the police. The police came and quieted things down. They took us off to where the dressing rooms were, locked us in, and left a policeman to guard the door. Now the rest of the show starts, the young comedian comes out, and he lasts about six minutes. The kids are all screaming, "Billy, Billy, Ricky, Ricky." It's hard to believe, really. So, he bails after six minutes because it just wasn't going anywhere. The Hootin' Annies came out and played to a lukewarm response. Then Beverly did her show and was fine but certainly deserved much more than what she got from the audience.

I felt so bad—the kids threw cold water on the evening, as I expected would happen. So now the crowd lets out and the cop opens the door and he used a very derogatory term. "Okay, you Jersey j------s, out!" There was a big tour bus outside and the performers were getting ready to leave.

I went over to the young comedian and apologized. I said, "Gee, I am really sorry, man."

He graciously said, "Don't worry about it, man. You were great." It was *Richard Pryor*. He was a skinny kid with a suit and tie, squeaky clean comedian, great little guy.

When I got back from the war, I was home about six months and was watching *The Dean Martin Show* on television one night and this kid comes on. He looked so familiar. Finally, I said, "Oh, my god, that's the kid from the Ice Palace."

The Jersey Beatles did fizzle out. We almost got killed. A lot of tough neighborhood guys hated The Beatles for what they stood for, and The Jersey Beatles were no exception. It wasn't all screaming girls and adulation, by any means. For a short time, the brother of one of Ricky's girlfriends, a pretty Puerto Rican girl named Leona, wanted to act as our manager. He would drive us around to various bars and nightclubs that had entertainment and go in and ask if they would allow The Jersey Beatles to perform a few songs. Most of the time it was fun. We were a novelty, and it worked well.

Then we went into this one Mafia club in Long Branch. I knew it was a mob club. I knew about some of the people there who were the actual people portrayed in *The Sopranos*, including Pussy Russo (Genovese crime family member Anthony "Little Pussy" Russo), among others. I remember as we were walking to the stage with our guitars, the bandleader said, "Well, ladies and gentlemen, we're going to take a short break, but while we're on break, we have a guest appearance tonight by The Jersey Beatles. Incidentally, the real Beatles were here last night, and they got stretched."

So, we're playing two songs and I noticed some milling around in the back of the room and I didn't like it. Between songs, I said quietly to Rick, "Look, don't worry about the car. After the last song, let's not get friendly with the crowd. Let's go to the door, get out of here, and run."

He said, "Why?" I said, "Don't worry about why. Just follow me." We played our last song, packed up our guitars, and we get outside. Sure enough, a whole carload of guys come around the block, screaming, cursing. They chased us for several blocks. We were running for our lives between houses, under clotheslines and railroad cars.

Finally, we reached Tony's Pizzeria, where we knew the guy. We used to play our guitars in there. We told Tony what happened, and he said, "Oh my God, those guys? Quick, get in the freezer." So, there we were, two frozen Jersey Beatles hoping we were out of trouble. We heard the guys come in and Tony said, "No, I haven't seen them." They left and then Tony opened the trunk of his car.

"Okay, you idiots," he said. "Get in the trunk. I'm going to drive you guys a few miles and let you out. Then, you're on your own."

We were curled up in the trunk of Tony's car and I looked at Ricky and Ricky looked at me and we knew it was inevitable. "It's time," I said, "for The Jersey Beatles to retire, WHILE WE STILL HAVE THUMBS!"

SIX

Writing for The Duprees and Kama Sutra Records

IN THE SPRING OF 1965 AFTER CASING BROADWAY FOR two years trying to get in the door, I got a call one night about 8:00 p.m. from Artie Ripp at Kama Sutra Productions in New York. I was living in a twenty-two-dollar-a-week motel room out on the Asbury Circle and putting up television antennas to keep myself alive. Rick went on to produce The Shannons, a very good local girl group. I was running to New York every week with my songs, hoping to get them published and recorded.

Ricky and I had co-written a song called "When" that we taught to the group to add to their show. The girls learned our song, and it was working well in their live performances. Around that time, the spring of '65, the Monmouth Mall in Eatontown, New Jersey, had their grand opening. It was a big event. They organized a rock and roll show in one of the parking lots to entertain the huge crowd. Jay and the Americans and The Shangri-Las were the co-headliners, and both groups were produced by Kama Sutra Productions in New York.

The promoters wanted some local acts, also, so they put The Shannons on the bill, and they sang our song. The guys from Kama Sutra were there and asked the girls, "Where did you get that song?"

"Our little friend, Billy Terrell, wrote it with our producer," the girls said.

"Well," they said, "we want you to come to New York and meet Artie Ripp."

Artie Ripp was an experienced producer who had worked with some of the best, including Don Kirshner. So they went up and they auditioned for Ripp, who asked the girls the same question: "Where did you get that song?"

"Our friend Billy wrote it with our producer," they said, and they gave him the name of the motel I was living at. About two or three days after that, at about eight o'clock at night, I was home writing because I'd write every night. I'd put up television antennas during the day and I'd write my songs at night. I got a call and it was Artie Ripp at Kama Sutra. It was the call I'd been waiting for—it seemed forever.

"Are you Billy Terrell?"

"Yes, why? Who's calling?"

"Well, did you write this song, 'When'?"

"Yessss," I said slowly.

"We would like you to come up and talk to us, because we would like to hear all your songs. We really think you've got talent."

I got chills when I heard that.

"Well, that's great," I said. I could hardly believe it. I had been knocking on doors for a couple years, trying to sell myself and my songs. And here, out of the blue, I get this call. I took the bus into New York, and as I walked down Broadway passed the Brill Building with its big brass doors, I got a chill. This was what I was hoping for.

Artie Ripp signed me to a fifty-dollar-a-week contract as a songwriter. The fifty-dollar-a-week contract was popularized by Don Kirshner and his partner, Al Nevins, who owned Aldon Music, which existed only from 1958 through 1963 but published more than two hundred hits. What they were doing was, they were grooming songwriters. Until then, a songwriter would knock on a publisher's door in the Brill Building or down the street at 1650 Broadway, where Kama Sutra had an office, and hope for a chance to present and sell their songs. If a publisher was in the mood, he'd listen, and if he liked a song, he'd buy it for twenty-five or fifty dollars, and he might even offer a bonus if the song got recorded by a known artist.

But Kirshner and Nevins had another idea. If they met a songwriter with promise, they wanted to tie them up with a deal that worked for everyone. They would pay the songwriters a "salary" of fifty dollars a week and give them a space to work, which was nothing more than a cubicle with a piano, a bench, and an ashtray. The weekly salary was really an advance against future royalties the songwriter would earn. The contract was usually for five years and was a win-win. The songwriter would have steady income and a place to work and bounce ideas off other writers, while Kirshner and Nevins could publish everything the songwriter produced for the next five years.

When Kirshner insisted on signing Neil Sedaka and his partner, Howie Greenfield, in 1958 (against Nevins' objections: "They look like pishers," Nevins protested), Kirshner's gamble immediately paid off with the duo writing huge hits for Connie Francis, followed by Sedaka's own hits as an artist. But when Kirshner signed Carole King and Gerry Goffin to a similar contract, it took that pair nearly eighteen months before turning a hit—but what a hit it was! "Will You Love Me Tomorrow" went right to number one in January of '61 for The Shirelles and was the first number one hit for a girl group since The Chordettes scored with "Mr. Sandman" seven years earlier.

So the Kama Sutra guys offered me a similar deal. It was tight, but I jumped at the opportunity. I had to sleep at the office a few nights a week because I couldn't afford to commute. I practically lived on coffee and donuts, but it was worth it.

The tenth floor at 1650 Broadway was amazing. Right next door to Kama Sutra was Cloud Nine Productions with a very young team, including Richard Perry, who became one of the great producers in the record business. Down the hall were the young team of Charles Koppelman and Don Rubin, who became the biggest publishers in the business. All of them were hustling and mostly all were struggling. Songwriter Wes Farrell was writing for Diamond Records on another floor and was dating record mogul George Goldner's daughter, who was the receptionist at Kama Sutra. For me, a young, inspired kid who left school after the ninth grade, it was a million-dollar education.

One evening Frankie Valli came to visit with Kama Sutra partner Hy Mizarhi, and I asked him for his autograph. "That kid is the next Phil Spector," Hy told Frankie. Things were happening fast, and it felt great.

The Duprees, who were recording for Columbia Records, sang the first song I had recorded. Kama Sutra needed a B-side for The Duprees. Artie handed me a tape of a track that was originally cut for The Shangri-Las and told me Columbia wanted to rush the record out. The A-side, "Around the Corner," sounded like a sure winner. He said to me, "Look, it's five o'clock in the afternoon and we have a session at seven and we've got to have a B-side. Take this track, write a song to it, and meet us at Columbia Studios." I walked in there at seven o'clock and I taught The Duprees the song. They recorded the song "They Said It Couldn't Be Done." It was June of 1965. That was my first recorded song, a B-side of a top twenty record.

Then they recorded me on a song that I wrote called "Do It My Way." I was like a Freddy Cannon-type record guy. Freddy Cannon had a big, bouncy hit called "Palisades Park." So they were grooming me as a writer and producer, and they recorded me at Allegro Studios in the basement of 1650 Broadway. One day, Artie called me into his office to ask me to listen to a new record that they were being pitched. It was an unmixed version of "Do You Believe in Magic" by a new group they discovered called The Lovin' Spoonful. They asked me what I thought of it.

"Well, it's either going to be the biggest thing or it's going to fail." I never heard anything like it. I just loved the record. The Lovin' Spoonful debuted on Billboard's Hot 100 with the song, which peaked at number nine. It has been a cult hit forever since then. It also marked the start of a great career for the group.

MGM offered the Kama Sutra guys their own label with MGM distribution. They told MGM, "We think we have the next forces in the music business. We just signed a group called The Lovin' Spoonful and they've got a great record, and this guy (John) Sebastian writes beautifully. We also have a band called The Hassles, and that piano player Billy Joel is killing it, and we've got this kid Billy Terrell that we're grooming as an artist and producer that we think is going to be very important."

Even though I only spent a little more than two months at Kama Sutra before being drafted, I learned an awful lot. I learned enough to know that this was the life I wanted, and I was going to stick with it no matter what. Fortunately for me, there was still enough innocence in popular music on the radio so that playing three or four chords on the guitar wasn't a problem. I was completely dedicated to co-writing as much as possible and taking advice and guidance from Hy Mizrahi and Artie Ripp at Kama Sutra. They gave me assignments mostly writing songs to existing music tracks that were intended for The Shangri-Las or other acts they were working with. I didn't want to disappoint them.

I was in with the in crowd at 1650 Broadway, the Mecca of rock and roll. I wouldn't trade those memories for anything. I remember Neil Diamond, Bobby Bloom, Wes Farrell, Jay and The Americans, The Shangri-Las, The Duprees all attending late night parties at the office. I was just a fly on the wall for those events. I had no interest in participating in the madness. A wild guy named Tony Bruno was a real character. He got drunk and challenged Artie Ripp to stand out on the window ledge and stay still for ten seconds. We were on the tenth floor, for God's sake! I went downstairs for coffee. I couldn't watch it. It was total insanity.

I was so dedicated, I used to sleep at the office several nights a week. I couldn't afford to go back and forth anyway, so I would write pretty much all night, sleep on a couch in one of the offices, and wash up in the men's room down the hall. One night I went down for coffee and locked myself out of the office. I couldn't believe it. I had no money and nowhere to go. There was a wonderful black man named Hank that was the night manager of the building. Really great guy. He felt sorry for me and allowed me to sleep in the stairwell on the first floor and kept an eye on me all night. Try that one today.

Having an opportunity to work with Shadow Morton was a wonderful experience. He wrote and produced The Shangri-Las' songs. Singing background on a session for him was a milestone for me at the time. Recording at Allegro Studios in the basement where so many hits were made was a dream come true. Being introduced to Frankie Valli as the next Phil Spector was overwhelming. It was those moments that helped establish my commitment to succeed. I was thrilled, but it didn't last. It wasn't long before I got my draft notice. I went to war knowing—at least believing—I had something really to live for and come home to. It kept me going through the worst of times.

When I was younger, I was watching the Cold War unfold. I was very frightened from a very young age and it affected me all through the '50s. I remember seeing the first televised atomic bomb test in April 1952. I was watching television that had a little screen. Nobody had big TVs then. I saw this massive explosion and I was dumbfounded. A few days later, I remember my mother saying to my brother, "Richie, where did

Billy go?" They're looking all over the house for me, and Richie said, "He's over there." I was hiding behind the couch, hugging my sister's doll, all hunched over, frightened. It freaked me out. That image stayed in my mind that whole time.

I also remember, several nights in Newark during the Korean War, they used to have blackouts where the rule was everyone in town had to turn the lights out in case of an attack—most likely by the Soviet Union, I suppose. The Koreans couldn't make it to Newark. I remember sitting in the kitchen in the dark. That freaked me out, that image, and then the bomb blast on TV.

All through the '50s, I would pay attention. I would listen to President Eisenhower whenever he would come on. I would be upset whenever he had a press conference, because I was convinced that he was going to declare war. I knew about our problems with the Soviet Union and, of course, the Space Race. I knew the whole *Sputnik* deal. I felt a strong connection to World War II and the horrors of it, all the way through to the early '60s.

When I got my draft notice, the guys at Kama Sutra did everything they could to convince me not to report. Before I had to report they called me up and—this is so stupid—they ran a séance to try and convince me not to go.

"Billy," they said, "we don't want you going to the war. You're going to ruin your career." So, they took me in one of the rooms we used to write in. They had a black light in there and they turned out all the lights and they had this beatnik priest from Greenwich Village with a big gong, and he's banging on this gong and he's talking in tongues. Then Monti Rock III comes in. He was a famous hairdresser, a crazy Hispanic hairdresser, and a very flamboyant guy. He had hair all the way to the floor, and he had a ribbon in it. He was sort of a hairdresser to the stars and he gained fame with appearances on *The Merv Griffin Show* at first and then *The*

Tonight Show. They made me sit on the floor and cross my legs and Monti Rock stood over me and pulled the ribbon out of his hair and it fell to the floor all around me. I'm sitting there in a Monti Rock hair tent with this beatnik banging the gong, talking in tongues, and they're telling me, "You can't go. You're going to put women's bloomers on. And you're going to put a dead fish in there. When you go for the physical and you take your clothes off and you're standing there in women's underwear, with a dead fish, there's no way they're going to put you in the army."

I stood up and I turned the lights on and I said, "Well, let me tell you something, guys. Look, my grandfather, the greatest guy in the world, came here with nothing in 1902 and worked hard and made it possible for me to be born an American. There's no way I could ever live with turning the country down for my service and, if I don't make it, I don't make it, but I got to serve. I appreciate everything you're trying to do for me. If I make it, I'll come back. What's going to be is going to be."

I didn't realize what a compliment it was that the Kama Sutra team was paying me—they thought that highly of me that they wanted to keep me alive and working with them. It was truly my big break, but I got up and walked out, and then I went into the army.

My father tipped me off to the draft earlier that year. He watched the news every night, so he knew something was brewing. It was obvious he was visibly nervous. I was twenty years old and eligible for the draft.

I wasn't paying attention to anything in the news at that time. I was living in a twenty-two-dollar-a-week motel room, putting up television antennas during the day to survive and writing music at night. Then, as it got closer to the spring, when LBJ escalated the war, I was in the first wave. I got hit with it all at one time.

SEVEN

They Drafted the Dregs

I GOT THE DRAFT NOTICE THE FIRST WEEK OF JUNE or the end of May. I was supposed to report the first week in July. Unfortunately, my grandfather passed, which was absolutely devastating to me. So they changed the date to August 5, because I was totally wiped out. No one I was ever close to had died before, let alone someone in my family. I barely knew my grandmother on my mother's side. But, Grandpa Torsiello's death was the most horrible thing. It just wrecked me.

I remember all the draftees had to go down to Asbury Park to the draft board down at 620 Bangs Avenue. I went down, reported for the draft, and then a bus took a bunch of us to Newark, New Jersey. I remember the ride very well. It was a very hot day. Probably about ninety-five degrees and the smell on the bus was awful. We were all the expendables. It was all the poor kids on that bus: black boys (we called them colored boys back then), uneducated whites, and Hispanics. And it was heartbreaking. We were obviously considered the dregs.

I mean, I was proud to serve. I wanted to serve. I never gave it a second thought about serving, but I knew right away that if you were in college, even if you were studying art, you were deferred. There were guys in the neighborhood that married girls that they didn't even like, because if you were married, you were out.

We had nowhere to go. I wouldn't have beat it anyway. That's just where my head was, so I had no problem. I wanted to; I was happy to serve. It was very painful because those faces—I can still see the faces. It was so obvious, right off the bat. We were the expendables. That's when the whole Vietnam thing really started sinking in. I didn't know much about the war, but it all started to sink in that this was different.

Yes, this was different! This was not World War II, where everybody ran out to sign up. This was selective service. They were throwing us to the wolves here. Then we got to the induction center and you really got a full dose of it there. You realized that they were going after what they considered the dregs and we didn't matter. We didn't matter, and we knew it.

At the induction center, it was crazy. Most of us were just standing in line waiting to be examined like it was just another day. Some totally off-the-wall people walked in doing anything possible to get rejected and sent home. The craziest was a tall guy with a winter overcoat, a Russian-style fur hat, snow boots, a scarf, and an upright bass. It was August 5th and ninety-five degrees for God's sake! He stood against a wall and started playing the bass and wouldn't stop or speak a word. Several people working there attempted to get the guy to say something, and stop playing the bass, but he wouldn't budge. They finally took him into a room and closed the door. We could hear the doctors yelling at the guy, but he never said a word or stopped playing the bass. They finally let him go. It was insane.

A few guys were let go for various medical reasons, but most of us were loaded on buses shortly after our examinations and taken to Fort Dix in South Jersey. The first few days we just hung around until they assigned us to basic training units. In the meantime, we had to cut the grass and pick up cigarette butts and stuff like that. A few guys wanted out no matter what. Even my close friend Ralph Marra said to me he didn't think he could make it. He did fine, though. He lucked out and was assigned to Okinawa in June of '66 instead of 'Nam. The worst was a guy named Poole. We were cutting the grass together with very old lawn mowers that were open at the top. Poole was really acting weird that day.

He said to one of the sergeants, "I'll take a dishonorable discharge."

"You can't request a dishonorable discharge," the sergeant told him. I'm out there cutting the grass and Poole is next to me and he taps me on the shoulder.

"I'm getting out of here," he tells me.

I said, "You're going to start that again? They drafted us, man."

"Hey," he said, "I just thought about this. How are they going to send me to Vietnam with no trigger finger?" A minute later he took the first finger on his right hand, stuck it down in the mower, and cut it off. Blood everywhere. We never saw him again.

In basic training, the vast majority of us were all uneducated, drafted kids, and we were treated like that. If you got real tired out, you'd get kicked or you'd get smacked or you'd have to go and run in circles. There was this one sergeant who would always torment people. He'd always say, "You guys will never make it. You'll die. I can tell. I can always tell. You guys will never last." Yes, they would intimidate us something awful.

The next eight weeks we trained in very hot weather. It was strange because it was obvious that most of us were living better than we were used to. We had three meals a day, got plenty of exercise, and were proud to serve. I personally felt like I was important and my life meant something. I felt equal. There were very few guys from affluent families that were volunteers and were decent people that didn't look down at me.

Then, I did a second eight weeks at Fort Dix, advanced infantry training. After the second eight, me and some other guys were sent down to Fort Lee, Virginia, to quartermaster school. My friend Reed from Conshohocken,

Pennsylvania, was with me from Fort Dix through Fort Lee all the way to 'Nam. We did a quartermaster course together that was four or six weeks. At the end of the course, it was the end of January, and they let everyone know where we were going, obviously 'Nam. We had a date to ship out. Then the night before, about midnight, two sergeants and an MP came in the barracks and they woke us up. They woke me and Reed and a couple of other guys and said, "Get your stuff. We're moving on."

"Well, we're not leaving until tomorrow," I said to him.

"You guys are leaving now. Come on."

So, we didn't leave with everybody. They put us on a train and they would not tell us where we were going. A day and a half later, we wound up in Kansas, and we joined the 96th Quartermaster in Fort Riley. That was a battalion.

It wasn't until I got to Fort Riley, Kansas, in late January 1966 that reality set in. A lot of the guys were assigned to the 96th Quartermaster battalion, as well as other logistical units, because they were convicted of serious crimes and given two options: (1) long prison terms, or (2) go to the army and on to Vietnam. The army obviously knew they couldn't discipline them enough out on the line. I remember one guy from the Bronx who was convicted of attempted murder back home stabbed another guy over at Junction City just before we had to ship out. When the doctors were certain the guy would survive, the army sent our guy back to our unit and on to 'Nam.

At Fort Riley, I became the mail guy, in addition to other duties, which was cool. We trained in the hills with the 1st Infantry Division playing simulated war games and learning a lot about the tactics of the Viet Cong. They trained us how to defend ourselves on convoys and what we should look for, as the enemy were always going to try to knock the supply routes off.

We trained with different weapons, and it was very cold too. We were sleeping in sleeping bags on the ground out there. It was, like, eighteen degrees in the morning when you got out of that sleeping bag and, my God, you were freezing to death. We used to be assigned to these guard posts during war games. I remember I was on this one guard post on a road far from our makeshift camp. I was out there for about fourteen hours and I was freezing. Finally, a truck came by and they said, "The games are over. Come on, we've done enough for today, come back." When I got back to camp, I was shivering. The first sergeant came over to me with another guy.

"Where were you?" he asked me.

"I'm freezing. I was out on the road post a few miles down. I've been out there fourteen hours."

"Well, why so long?"

"Well, nobody relieved me. I wasn't going to walk off guard."

"That's a good man," the other sergeant said.

"Yes, a frozen man."

I used to hang out in Manhattan, Kansas, on the weekends, which was a nice little town. That's where Kansas State University is located. They had a little college town close to the campus called Aggieville. They had coffeehouses there with the peanuts on the floor, in the shells. I used to go there and play guitar and write. I liked to hang out at Tuttle Creek sometimes, also, and there was a place called Delmonico's in Ogden, Kansas, right outside the base. I used to go there many nights to sit in and play with the band. We were soldiers preparing for war during the day, but I was all music after hours and on weekends. In Kansas, especially in Manhattan, it was okay.

So we finally got orders for Vietnam. I remember the last night. They gave us this big orientation. They said, "We're not telling you exactly where you're going. You can't talk to anybody about any of this and nobody can leave the base." Well, I snuck off the base. I was a good discipline guy, but I had to go to Delmonico's and play one more time. So I snuck off the base and worked my way down to Delmonico's. I was in there playing and one of the sergeants that wasn't supposed to be off the base either walked in.

"You're not supposed to be here," he said.

"Sergeant, I thought about it, and I said to myself, *What are you going to do, send me to Vietnam?*"

He said, "Well, I'm not telling if you're not."

"We better just enjoy the music and sneak back on the base and be done with it," I said. And that's exactly what we did.

They flew the whole battalion to Oakland, California. I remember the Red Cross was there with coffee and donuts at the pier. We got on the troopship called the USS *Walker*. I recently found out that the *Walker* went back and forth, dumping troops, coming back, dumping more troops, and retuning. We were one of the earlier groups that went there. We got on as a battalion and we sailed from Oakland to Tacoma, Washington, and picked up more troops there. The USS *Walker* was built in 1944. I remember my buddy Reed. I was with him pretty much through the whole thing, from basic into Lee and Fort Riley. I remember being on the deck of the ship going under the Golden Gate Bridge and somebody had a small transistor radio. "A Groovy Kind of Love" was playing, by The Mindbenders. It was the first hit song written by both Carole Bayer Sager and Toni Wine.

"Wouldn't you agree, baby, you and me, got a groovy kind of love."

"Take a good look," I said to Reed, "because we might not see this again."

I just kept looking back at America. Then we went up to Tacoma, picked up a few thousand more guys and started to zigzag across the Pacific.

EIGHT

All Mothers Cry the Same Color Tears

WE LEFT TACOMA, AND IT WAS CRAZY ON THAT SHIP, because, oh God, we ran out of water and the food was just awful, god-awful! In the morning they served these horrible powdered eggs, and the milk went sour. You used to stand in line and, by the time you got your breakfast, you'd have to go stand in line again for lunch. It got so bad that they had armed guards at the door downstairs near the pantries where the cooks were. They would put everything on a dumbwaiter and it would come up to the big dining area on the ship.

The food was so bad, and we had to do something out there. I got together with a bunch of guys and I came up with the brainstorm. I was always the guy who would come up with the schemes. So I said to Reed, "Look, I've got an idea. You take a mailbag and go down in the dining room and stand by the dumbwaiter." It was so stupid; we were in the middle of the ocean.

"I'm going to take a mailbag," I told him, "and I'm going to go down below and I'm going to ask the armed guards if they have any mail to go out and tell them I'd like to go down into the kitchen and pantry area to see if there was anybody that had any mail down there."

They all start writing letters furiously. They're all writing quick letters to put in the bag and I'm dying because I'm thinking, *What do they think*

I'm going to do with the mail? We're in the middle of the freaking ocean. But what it did, it allowed me time alone in the pantry. I was putting food on the dumbwaiter and banging on it and Reed was taking it upstairs. I collected all the mail and said, "Thanks, guys." Reed and I went back to our cabin, where we didn't have cots but instead we had three rows of hammocks. We slept practically on top of each other. What a drag that was, because the food made you pass a lot of gas and I don't want to tell you how horrible that was, sleeping under one of those maniacs in a hammock. Well, when Reed and I went below and dumped that food out, the guys went crazy. We had a feast.

The other scheme I had was great. We noticed that the officers all ate on an upper deck. They had their dinners up there and that food was much better than our food—*much, much* better. On the ship they had some music instruments, which gave me the idea. So, I approached one of the officers.

"Lieutenant Manion, I'm hooking up some entertainment," I told him. "There are some guys on the ship beside me that also play instruments. We're going to work up some songs and we were thinking maybe the officers up there one night would like to hear some music. We can come up there, play music, and maybe we could get something decent to eat."

"Well, you know what?" he said. "That's a fair tradeoff. Why don't you see what you can do?"

We were dreadful, oh, my God, it was so bad. We went up there to play and we were awful. We had that certain NOTHING! The Beatles had a big song called "Nowhere Man," so I called the band The Nowhere Men. We're up there and we're playing and we're eating the whole time. We're also putting food in our pockets to take back to our buddies. While we were on a short break, an officer from one of the other companies came over to me.

"Hey, what's the name of that band?"

"We're the Nowhere Men," I said.

"Oh, yes, you're right on that one," he cracked, and he walked away.

But the kicker was we ate like kings.

After about twenty-some days zigzagging, we finally see the outline of the shore of Vietnam. Our first stop was Quy Nhon, a large port and airbase for the U.S. That's where I wound up in the hospital in December that year. We pulled into the Quy Nhon area and we had some Vietnamese coming towards our ship on these flat-bottomed wooden boats called sampans. We were well armed. They told us to stand away from the edge, in case there were bad guys who would pick somebody off or maybe throw a grenade or something on top of the ship. Fortunately, that wasn't the case.

We let off one whole battalion at Quy Nhon and then sailed to Cam Ranh Bay and got off there. They didn't tell us anything about it. All we knew was that we were going into a war zone. They didn't tell us that Cam Ranh Bay, at that time, was a very, very safe place. It was really an island. There wasn't a lot of water between the perimeter and the mainland, but it was isolated enough and relatively safe. There were mountains at the beach and the base was beyond those mountains, but we didn't know that. They put us on these boats called LSUs (for Landing Ship Utility) that took us ashore. This platform would lower, and you'd jump off, just like in World War II.

We were all loaded up with gear. The M14 was eleven pounds and I was just 117. You had to jump into the water with the M14 and ammo and all your stuff. One guy almost drowned. We're standing on the beach, and we're in formation. They didn't tell us that engineers were working on putting a communication tower on one of the hills. They didn't tell us much of anything about the area.

We're standing out there waiting for trucks to come pick us up when, all of a sudden, a massive explosion takes place. They blew the top off one of the mountains to build a pad up there. We were so jumpy, we ran back in the water like dummies. It was terrible. After we got over that fiasco, we were in Cam Ranh Bay for a couple of days. It was safe, and the food wasn't bad there. Then they broke us up into smaller units. Company A stayed in Cam Ranh Bay, but Company B was redesignated the 226th Supply and Service, and they put us on trucks. We went to Phan Rang, which was an entirely different environment.

That was our first convoy. We were on the back of the two-and-a-half-ton trucks. There was a lead jeep with a lieutenant in the lead. It was pretty much like the scene in the 1987 film *Good Morning, Vietnam* when those deuce-and-a-halves were going to Nha Trang. I remember we pulled out and we were on a road and that was our first taste of Vietnam. I remember the guy sitting next to me. We had on our flak jackets and steel pots and we were locked and loaded, ready for anything.

"Suddenly, Vietnam becomes Vietnam," I remember the young fellow sitting next to me saying.

"I'm afraid so," I agreed.

Fortunately, we didn't have trouble on that convoy, but that was the first one. It was very scary, though. We had been in Cam Ranh a couple of days. We were walking around at night in our shorts and there was ice cream down there and stuff. Then we got our orders, were loaded on these trucks, and were sent down these roads into the jungle. We're looking in the trees for snipers and hoping we're not going to hit any landmines. It was a frightening first convoy.

When we arrived in Phan Rang, it was scary because it was obvious we were very vulnerable. High brush and thick forest were all around our camp. It was so dark at night you couldn't see your hand in front of your face. We feared we might shoot another American by mistake. Phan Rang was a scary place. We were sitting ducks there, especially at night. I slept with my M14, with a round in the chamber and the safety on. All I would have to do is click the safety off and let her go. We put up tents and had folding cots to sleep on. We also had to wrap mosquito nets completely around ourselves as we slept. The bugs were bad. We had to deal with crawly things coming out of the high grass.

One morning I woke up to find a scorpion crawling over the net protecting my face. Right over my face! I had to lie very still. A couple guys got around me, and they said, "Just don't move." They started this little fire, and then they grabbed the net and—*shoop*—they threw the whole net into the fire and burned the net and the scorpion.

We had one little building that they built on the perimeter which was like a little enlisted men's service club with beer and stuff. It was a makeshift wooden shack with a small bar and few tables. Outside, we had a bright light in the back illuminating the heavy bush on the perimeter to prevent the Viet Cong from getting too close without being noticed. I hung out at that club every night even though I didn't drink.

We had some rough times in Phan Rang. One night all hell broke loose. It was so stupid. There was a monkey that climbed up on the captain's tent and one of the guys shot it, I guess for kicks. It sent everyone running to get their weapons. It was so dark the only thing I could do was lie still in high grass and not panic. I felt footsteps running past me, so close it's a miracle I wasn't stepped on. There was no way to determine if they were our guys or VC, so I didn't shoot, thank God! Fortunately, shortly after that incident, toward the end of July, our company got orders to move to Tuy Hoa, which was farther north and closer to the coast. Once we were settled there, somebody came up from Phan Rang with horrifying news.

"You guys will never believe this—they blew that club up. The VC got close enough to blow that club up with all those guys in it."

If it happened a month earlier, we would have been finished. That was a tough pill to swallow. If we hadn't moved to Tuy Hoa, I probably would have perished. It still gives me chills.

As far as assignments go, we did a variety of things. We processed supplies. I was the mail guy, but there wasn't much mail. Then everybody had perimeter guard. No matter what your job was, you pulled a certain amount of guard duty to protect the perimeter, mostly at night. You're out there, and you're hoping and praying that you're not going to get picked off. There were some nasty times on perimeter guard.

Working on convoys taking stuff from one place to another was extremely dangerous. That was no walk in the park, because you never knew what was going to happen. We had one lieutenant that had such a bad nervous breakdown, they sent him home. Lucky him. It was kind of confusing, the day-to-day activity, because it just never seemed like we were getting anywhere. Even in the early days, it seemed that way. I used to say to myself, "Okay, well, that's another day." You lived for that next sunrise. All you'd think about was getting through that one day and seeing another sunrise. It was a day at a time. Every morning the sun came up, it reminded you that your mother was spared another day.

There were many problems in Tuy Hoa, as racial tensions were astronomical. It was painful hearing about illegal killings going on in some of the other units in our area. It didn't make any sense to be wasting each other. One of the most horrible abuses I witnessed was one of our guys, who was obviously homosexual, being raped. I really wanted to kill those guys that did that. It was awful. I went back to my hooch, put a round in the chamber, and finally talked myself out of it. But it was close. At that point, the entire experience was catching up with me. I'd had enough.

The one lesson that I did learn in Vietnam that prevented me from murdering someone was all mothers cry the same color tears. It was our mothers that suffered the worst. It didn't matter what your job was. More importantly, it was no comfort to any one of our mothers, because all they knew was that their son was in a war. You walked out the door at home and that was it.

It was totally unlike today. God bless these soldiers today, with technology. My young sister's son graduated from West Point. He was a captain with the 101st Airborne in Iraq and Afghanistan. Once a week, he talked to my sister on Skype. In our war, however, you walked out that door, you hugged your mother, and you either walked back in a year later or they handed her a folded flag.

NINE

The Orphanage at Tuy Hoa

FOR MY OWN SAFETY, I CONVINCED THE COMPANY commander to let me make my own dwelling. What I did was, I created a mailroom out of a Conex container. A Conex container is made of steel and is about five feet square and six feet high with a heavy door. I put up these tin cans and labeled them alphabetically for sorted mail. I wrote to Monmouth College in New Jersey in September of '66 and I told them who I was and asked them to ask students if they would be kind enough to write letters addressed to the boys of the 226th Supply and Service.

With Captain Bon's blessings, I used this steel Conex container for a makeshift mailroom.

LETTERS TO THE EDITOR

To The Editor:

I am a soldier serving with the 226th Supply and Service Compa- in Tuy Hoa, Vietnam.

I am the company mail clerk and I am having a rough time because the company isn't getting enough mail.

If it would be at all possible, I would appreciate some mail for my men from the students at your college.

Mail is the most important thing to GI in Vietnam and we just aren't getting enough. Being the mail clerk I think it's my job to take action and request that the students write.

It doesn't matter what they write about just the idea of geting mail from home is a great moral booster.

If you are able to help me out please address the mail to:

"TO THE BOYS OF THE" 226th SS Company Tuy Hoa Sub-Area CMD c-o Advisory Team No.28 APO San Francisco, Calif. 96316

The reason I chose Monmouth College is because I live only about 4 miles from the college in Wanamassa and I think a college of your size could help me a great deal.

Yours Truly, PFC William P Torsiello Mail Clerk 226th SS Co. APO 96316

This letter is in the archives at Monmouth College in New Jersey.

There's a copy of how that letter appeared above. I started getting tons of letters and I made sure that everybody got mail. When I used to go to outposts and firebases, I'd bring some supplies. For example, dry socks were in high demand. I used to bring mail and sometimes I'd barter for soda and ice. Ice was a delicacy. You could never drink the ice, because the ice was contaminated, but it would keep the cans cold. You had to wash the cans off; if you left that ice water there, you could get malaria, which eventually I did. I used to scrounge up some ice from some of the locals and put it in a container and I'd put some Cokes in there and I'd go to a firebase. They'd be firing off these 105s. It got so hot and we would sweat so intensely that by the end of the day our uniforms would have long white powder streaks down our backs and both arms. It was salt we were losing from our bodies. I would take my bayonet and scrape one-inch mounds of salt from my sleeves. We had to take salt pills almost every day to compensate or we'd be in trouble. The hottest day I remember was 134 degrees one afternoon in Tuy Hoa in August '66. I could hardly breathe. It was miserable.

Whenever I arrived at an outpost or firebase, the guys would love seeing me show up with the mail. "Hey, guys," I'd holler, "I've got some mail from the college students. And, now, for an added bonus . . ."

"Drop off the stuff and get out of here," they'd holler at me.

"Wait a minute," I'd say, and I'd plop the bucket down. "Cold sodas!"

Oh, they used to go nuts. Cold sodas were a delicacy. The water in our canteens tasted terrible. If you didn't have Kool-Aid to put in it, you would gag drinking it. The guys at the fire bases would've gladly given a million dollars for one of my cold sodas and letter from home. I often wondered if any of those guys ever stayed in touch with those students.

Back in base camp, eventually, I was given permission to move into a tin shack that I lived in away from everybody. One reason was because it made no sense to me that some of the guys were hanging their flak jackets in our tent at night with hand grenades still attached. I quietly requested moving without giving up any names. Not a healthy thing to do in 'Nam. But nobody can throw a hand grenade that far to the perimeter and where are you going to throw it in the base camp? It's windy and with the monsoon, all we needed was a grenade going off and four or five of us were going to go home. The officer in charge agreed, and he let me live in my own hooch for the rest of my tour.

I got there at the end of May of '66 and I left May 29, '67, so one year. Lieutenant Scheer, who I've reunited with recently, was a real square guy. I served with him in Fort Riley, as well. He was a friend. I taught him how to play guitar over there.

Tuy Hoa was nothing when we first arrived. We were literally dug in. We had to dig holes and put the tents over them. Eventually, they built an airbase nearby and it got a lot safer.

I never made it to Saigon. I was never down there. I was always pretty much up north, and lived in a tent most of my time. There were no houses or anything. Then when I had the shack, that was a little bit better, but it was still a tin shack. Fortunately, we got out of Phan Rang when we did. We went down to the shore, we loaded everything on this navy ship, because Highway 1 was too dangerous to go from Phan Rang all the way to Tuy Hoa by convoy. They had gotten word it was just too far to travel safely. The enemy could have had plenty of time to dig in along the way, and we probably would've lost a substantial number of people.

We got on a navy ship that took us up to Tuy Hoa. We slept one night on the ship, which was heaven, because we were eating junk in the field. On the ship we slept in warm cabins out of the elements, and the mess hall was open twenty-four hours. I got up in the middle of the night and went down there and had more ice cream. They had ice cream and cold milk! Oh, I didn't want to get off the ship. I didn't want to go.

When we got to Tuy Hoa and we got off, I saw how desolate it was. The first thing we saw was a C-141 cargo plane that had crashed or had gotten shot down. There was debris everywhere. We had a lot of problems settling in, but we were blessed with Major Pruitt, who was there overseeing everything. Major Pruitt was a real stand-up guy. Then he almost died. He was in a Huey that was shot down. He survived, but we didn't see him again. We dug in up there and it took a while. As in Phan Rang, we lived in tents outside. Then when the monsoon season came in, that was a mess, because you were just wet all the time. All the time.

Three or four months of the monsoon seemed like forty-five years to me. It was wind and rain, and rain, and more rain. It just never got comfortable. Your feet were soaking wet all the time. After a few months, I became incredibly ill, and that threw me into a tailspin.

Lt. Scheer became one of my closest friends in Vietnam. He grew up in the north side area of Chicago and attended Loyola University of Chicago, where he enrolled in the ROTC program on campus and was commissioned as an army 2nd lieutenant in the Quartermaster Corps (QMC). At 6'5", he just missed being too tall to be accepted in the army. He had brown hair and hazel eyes and wore glasses, without which he would have been legally blind. Interestingly, he was four years into studying for the priesthood when he changed his mind. At Loyola he majored in English literature and minored in theology and philosophy. The day of his graduation he was also commissioned, and his mother and fiancée Carol each pinned a gold bar on one shoulder designating his rank as 2nd lieutenant. Three weeks later he reported for active duty.

He eventually was assigned to Tuy Hoa (about one hundred miles north of Cam Ranh Bay). At that point, he became the Class 1 (food storage depot) officer, in addition to his ongoing duties as graves registration platoon leader. This made sense, since he had the only generators and the only refrigeration in the area at that time. Here is how he first found out about the nuns and the poor orphans there.

One day two Vietnamese nuns came onto our camp rummaging for food. The nuns first were picking up C-ration cans from a ditch, trying to find food to feed the children. These cans were ready to be burned up because they were contaminated. We were eating left over C-rations from World War II—twenty-year-old food. Any cans that were dented were burned up. Lt. Scheer saw what was happening and he stopped the nuns from taking the cans. Here's how he explained it:

"One typically hot morning at my food storage and distribution depot, I was having my men bury bulging cans of food because they had gone bad. Suddenly, two nuns appeared at the depot gate and they were obviously begging for the spoiled food that we were disposing of. They spoke no English and we didn't speak Vietnamese, but I made it apparent that I couldn't give them that stuff. Instead, I opened my wallet and gave them ten dollars in military scrip.

Lieutenant Scheer with the kids.

"Several hours later, the same two nuns walked into our compound along with a priest who spoke a bit of English. He explained that these were two of six nuns who had been evacuated from the village of Tuy An, in Phu Yen Province, just before Mang Lang Orphanage was overrun by the North Vietnamese and Viet Cong. He said they were caring for about one hundred orphans and sick elderly people and that they had no suitable place to use for a mission."

He accompanied the priest and nuns back into the village of Tuy Hoa, where he saw the horrid conditions the kids where living under, piled up in a dirty wing of the small hospital. They were dirty and hungry. Cribs for infants and toddlers were set lengthwise against one wall with no space between each crib. What they needed was a building of their own.

"I told them I would do whatever I could to raise funds," said Lieutenant Scheer, "so they could build a proper orphanage. Since I was pay officer for my company (226th Supply & Service), I took the opportunity at the next payday to put out a cigar box labeled "For the Mang Lang Orphanage" and asked each person to contribute whatever they could spare for this worthy cause. Over the next two paydays, we accumulated enough funds to allow the nuns to purchase land and begin laying a foundation.

"However, I was impatient at the slow progress, so I wrote to Monsignor John B. Ferring, the pastor of St. Margaret Mary Parish in Chicago. This was the parish where I was born and raised. The very next Sunday, Msgr. Ferring took up a special collection at all the masses and raised six hundred dollars, which he sent me as a cashier's check. I was able to get this converted into the Vietnamese currency at a higher than normal rate, and this proved to be more than enough to build a two-story brick orphanage. I should also mention that a number of our enlisted men during their off-duty hours helped with construction of the building and others taught the children English and how to play baseball."

Then the local government stepped up and donated the rest of the land needed to get the project underway. It was a true blessing, for sure. Lieutenant Scheer deserves a humanitarian award for sure!

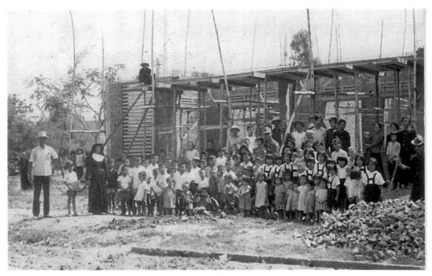

Early stage of construction of the new orphanage near Tuy Hoa in September 1966.

We got very attached to the children, and we were their safety net. I remember going down there one day after a really rough time on the road. I took an amazing picture. Well, the orphanage was under construction and only had these flat-board beds, no mattresses. There was a little girl there, about three years old, and her little brother was about six or seven months old. He's on his stomach and she was holding a bottle in his mouth. Both of their parents had been killed and their home torched by the VC. I captured that picture. I never let it out of my sight.

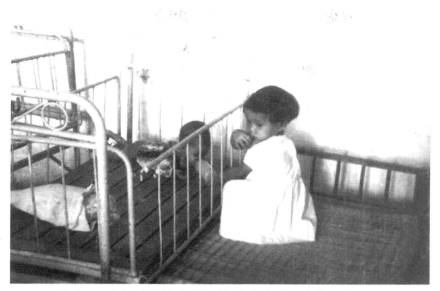

Heartbreaking seeing this child feed her baby brother at the orphanage.

Once the boys learned baseball, that's all they wanted to do whenever I visited.

Me and Johnny Young from Bayonne, New Jersey, just before we boarded the navy ship to move from Phan Rang to Tuy Hoa in July 1966.

Bonding with the children provided extraordinary moments of peace for us, as well, in spite of being in the midst of a horrific conflict.

During construction, several times a week various troops from our unit and others in the area would bring food to the children and spoonfeed them. I used to feed the children and I taught the boys how to play baseball. We also continued to bring money to the nuns during our pay periods. They loved us, and we loved them dearly. One day the Mayor of Tuy Hoa and another member of the city council came to the orphanage. The mayor was so moved he invited me and a few other guys to join him and his family for dinner, which we did a few nights later.

It was very pleasant. But the ride back to our base camp on Highway 1 late in the evening was a nightmare. There were four of us in a jeep moving as fast as we could go without sliding into the rice paddies on each side of the narrow dirt road. Then we noticed something blocking the road ahead. We ducked down, and the driver floored it. That caused those blocking the way to scatter and dive into the mud. We weren't sure if they were Viet Cong or just angry farmers. But one thing was for sure: they wanted us dead.

Many families lived in mud huts with straw roofs out in the middle of the paddies. They weren't concerned about politics or even who ran the country. Communism or democracy didn't seem to matter to them either way. They did resent us invading their space, even though our presence was for their advantage and overall well-being.

All in all, with the war raging in the highlands, the VC trying to pick off any Americans they could, and the local VC sympathizers working both sides of the game driving us crazy, one thing was for certain: the orphanage was not only a sanctuary of peace for our babies; they provided much more for us with their love and appreciation. Those were precious moments for us to step out to *the other side of war.*

I fed those babies and I taught a lot of the boys to play baseball. They loved baseball. My little buddy, Tung, was such a sweet little guy. They all wanted to be held and they were so affectionate. When I had to leave, it was devastating, because Tung would hold on so tight. They had to pry him off me, and he would scream bloody murder.

For years, I would hear those screams and I'd often wondered how they made out after the south fell. He would just want to be held all the time and play, but leaving was awful. He'd hyperventilate. It was heartbreaking. We did a lot of good for a lot of children because we truly cared. Those were the good memories. It's what helped maintain our sanity.

Me feeding the kids at Mang Lang Orphanage in September 1966.

Lt. Klempner at Mang Lang Orphanage in 1967.

My little buddy Tung was so great. He cried so bad every time
I had to leave that it haunted me for years.

Me and Sergeant Manual bringing money to Sister Theresa to help feed the children.

Lt. Klempner on the beach at Tuy Hoa with our guitars.

At Jordan Klempner's home in 2001. We've been as close as brothers ever since.

TEN

Two Refrigeration Units: One for Food and One for Bodies

HERE I WAS IN THE SUMMER OF '66, A PROMISING songwriter, serving in a war I didn't understand in the middle of Vietnam. I believed in fighting for my country, but I didn't believe in dying needlessly. When the 4th Division first got over there a few months after we arrived, they didn't seem to be well prepared. Their casualties early on were devastating. I didn't really understand it. I witnessed the horrible results of that. I would go to the 101st Airborne base a few clicks north of our base camp where they had a landing zone. Officially, I was the mail guy, and I'd be bringing them mail or other supplies and riding shotgun lots of times. Those roads were bad. Most of the time I would ride shotgun with my buddy Parham from Georgia. Great guy. I didn't drive a car back home until I was twenty-seven, but they needed drivers, so they asked me to.

"I don't drive," I told them.

"That's okay," they said. "Drive anyway."

I drove, but I wasn't very good at it, and it got bad on Highway 1. It got worse on those off roads. It wasn't fun and games in base camp either.

The 606th Ordinance lost people defusing munitions. They had guys that were specifically trained to defuse grenades and artillery shells. A few of their guys were careless and lost their lives in the process. Horrible site and sound. The enemy would manipulate any unexploded munitions into what is known today as IEDs (Improvised Explosive Devices). We called them booby traps back then. You'd hear that go off and, oh boy.

We had two refrigeration units—one for frozen foods and other foodstuff, and the other one was for bodies. That was the post-traumatic stress. I realize that a lot of my problems were survivor's guilt and seeing some of those boys taken in, especially the 101st Airborne. I'd be up there and those medevac choppers would be coming in. They had a small outpost there where the dustoff choppers brought casualties from the field for graves registration. That stayed with me. That never really left, seeing those ponchos lined up with the dead or near dead.

We had a graves registration platoon in our base camp, as well. Lieutenant Scheer was the officer in charge. Here's how he remembered it.

"We had eight enlisted men who did all the gathering and processing of bodies and body parts plus personal effects, which we then transported to Saigon for final processing before they were shipped to the States. Often the bodies were not just bloody but also mangled. In order to cope, we had to become automatons. Otherwise it would have driven us crazy."

I don't know how Lieutenant Scheer could stomach it day in and day out. I remember this one time out at the 101st outpost, a chopper landed, and they took the casualty off in a poncho. This one guy wasn't dead yet and I guess you had to be hardened to decide if he was too far gone. Someone came out from the bunker, looked in the poncho, and said, "Nah, he's over." He wasn't even dead yet! I could see over the side of the poncho that every time his heart beat, his blood was squirting over the side. It just seemed so cold, that they had to make those kinds of decisions. Guys were coming in left and right in those ponchos, all torn to pieces. It hit me so hard. I didn't sleep very well for a long time. The attitude seemed to be: *Oh, he's gone, let's get to the next one, put him in there, he'll never make it.* It never leaves you.

Then it was my turn. I got separated from my unit on a convoy when I became very ill. The (South) Korean troops who shared our base camp provided much security for us. I believe they were the ones who took me to the 563rd Medevac, which was a landing zone where casualties were taken initially to be stabilized. The 563rd was on a hill in North Tuy Hoa. They had one tent that provided shelter from the elements until a medevac chopper would come to take the wounded and sick to one of the field or evacuation hospitals, such as 8th Field in Nha Trang or the 67th Evac, which was on an airbase at Quy Nhon. I was in very bad shape. The tent was full, so they had me and a couple of the other guys wrapped up in ponchos outside the tent. We were lying in the rain overnight. I laid in the water. It was bad. The next day a chopper picked me up and took me first to the 67th Evac, where I was for a few days. Then they sent me down to 8th Field Hospital in Nha Trang. That was the army's only operating hospital in South Vietnam at the beginning of 1965, with a one hundred bed capacity. The building was also where Green Beret headquarters was. On the compound was an area they called Tent City. It was sandbags and tents, but they had much larger teams of medical doctors there because it was a heavy casualty hospital. By the time I got there, I was running a 105-degree fever and I was totally delirious.

I had still been doing my duty, though I felt weak for over a month and later learned I had malaria. I didn't know I had contracted double pneumonia too. I remember when they first brought me in, before they brought me over to the ICU, they left me for a minute while the next chopper came in. Four guys brought up a poncho and placed it right next to my bed, and to my shock, inside the bag was a young boy that had stepped on a landmine. Half of him had been torn apart. I couldn't even bear looking. It was awful. Just awful.

I was in such bad shape they had to throw me in a bin of ice because I was going to die. When they took my boots and my pants off, they saw that my skin was rotting off and my foot was so bad that there was a hole between my small toe on the right and the second one in. Between those toes, they were using wax suppositories with medication and they were sticking it all inside my foot. My foot was literally rotting off.

They came by and they gave me a shot. My face was all swollen up. I was a disaster. I was pitiful. I was delirious, totally delirious. I heard the doctor say, "I want you to check this guy's vitals every thirty minutes. I want you to give him a shot every hour. I want you to keep him cooled down and, if he makes it to the morning, I think we'll probably have a chance." I fought like crazy to not fall asleep.

It was December of '66, and coming up on the holidays, and in that ICU tent the Red Cross had a small row of Christmas lights along the border. I was lying there with my eyes almost swollen shut. I was just so miserable. All I could hear was the doctor saying, "Oh, shit."

I guess he thought I was gone at first. I was totally out of it. I must've said at least a hundred times, "What's my mother going to do if I don't make it? It'll kill her."

Finally, I passed out and the next day I saw a bright, blinding light from the other side of the tent. The sun was coming up over the sandbags shining right into my eyes. At first, I thought it was the light that you see when you're on your way to heaven, because I had heard the stories. I thought I was out of here. I remember struggling with thoughts of my mother, and then, finally, I realized it was the sun coming up.

It was coming up on the holidays and Martha Raye, who was a big movie and TV comedy star in the '40s and '50s, was there to help. She would do little comedy bits for us in between her duties as a nurse at the hospital. Then Cardinal Spellman, who was the Archbishop of New York, and Reverend Billy Graham came to visit the hospital. They were at my bedside. Billy Graham was holding my right hand and Martha Raye was holding my feet, and they all said prayers for me. Cardinal Spellman gave me last rites and put a crucifix on a chain around my neck for me as a gift. (When I was totally in the gutter after the war, I hocked it for the price of a drink.)

The late, great Martha "Colonel Maggie" Raye worked tirelessly, as all the nurses did in the field and evacuation hospitals in Vietnam. True angels.

Then, I went down to eighty-nine pounds, skin and bones. They used to have to force me to move my bowels. I had no muscle tone at all. I couldn't lift a spoon. They were trying to get me out of bed. I just couldn't do it. One day, Martha Raye came in and she rubbed my head and demanded I listen to her. "Troop, if you don't walk, you're going to die," she said. "And you're not going to die on my watch!"

She went around the back and she put her arms underneath my arms in a bear hug and she slid me out of bed and I was literally like Gumby. I was just flapping in the wind. I couldn't control anything.

"Now, damn it, stand on my feet," she demanded. She walked me back and forth, over and over. Then she came in another day and another day and she'd say, "Well, you're going for a walk now." It got my blood flowing, and then I started to recover. If it weren't for "Colonel Maggie," as we affectionately referred to her, I probably wouldn't have made it. While we were walking one day, I mentioned that my father was in show business and had played the Hotel Taft in New York in the early '40s before the war.

"Oh, we all played the Hotel Taft," she said. "Was he with (bandleader) Vincent Lopez?"

"Yes, I think so. I remember him mentioning Vincent Lopez," I said. "He also told me he worked with Joe Pica on piano in one of the smaller rooms, as well." She smiled and kept me walking.

By the time she introduced herself to me, Martha Raye had been working army hospitals for twenty-five years, all through World War II, Korea, and Vietnam. She was also a full-bird colonel in the Army Reserve. No celebrity ever gave more for their country.

Flashing forward, in the '80s, I was writing songs with a woman named Gloria Nissenson, who did a lot of Broadway stuff, and Ritchie Adams, who wrote the 1961 Bobby Lewis classic, "Tossin' and Turnin'." We had to cut one of our writing sessions short because Gloria said she had a show that was closing that night. Martha Raye was in the show and I wasn't aware.

"Martha Raye, she's in town?" I asked.

"Yes, but she's leaving tonight," she said.

"Oh, man. I've got to get a note to her." So, I wrote a letter explaining that I wouldn't have been alive if it hadn't been for her. Gloria promised to take it to her. In retrospect, I can kick myself for not going with her. A couple weeks passed, and Gloria came up to write again, and at that session I asked if she gave my letter to Martha Raye.

"Oh, yes," she said. "I gave it to her at the theater and she handed it to her manager and told him, 'Hang on to that. I want to read it in private.' After the performance, she went up to the dressing room and read the letter. She was tremendously moved by it and wept." I wish I could have thanked her in person. Deservedly, she was later honored with the Presidential Medal of Freedom.

Well, anyway, I was in the hospital the better part of a month. I thought they were going to send me home or send me to Okinawa and then home. They would've, but they kept me there on a technicality, because I wasn't in one hospital for more than thirty days. I was in three places, and they wouldn't combine it. So they sent me back out.

Quiet time in my hooch in 1967 in Tuy Hoa.

When I got back out to the field in January, I looked like I was in a concentration camp. That's when I first met and bonded with a young officer, Lieutenant Jordan Klempner, who was just twenty-one years old, from Brooklyn, New York. We played our guitars together many evenings to make it all bearable. We played in bunkers and the mess tent, but we weren't supposed to socialize at all, he being an officer and me being an enlisted man. Our friendship and mutual love for music helped us keep our sanity.

Then in May 1967, I was only nineteen days from coming home and I had one of my worst experiences in Vietnam. Lieutenant Klempner and I were ordered to go as an advance party up to Duc Pho, below Chu Lai. This was my last convoy—I was to be the bodyguard, riding shotgun!

We got on a chopper and flew up there to bring pay for some replacements coming in that were going to establish, outside Duc Pho, another place to bring supplies below Da Nang. I was afraid we were going to get shot down at one point, by the way the pilot was flying.

I found myself looking straight down at the ground as we were flying sideways. I'm saying, "Oh, please, I'm too short for this." (When you're short, you were a short-timer or had very little time left to serve.) "This is for a FNG [fucking new guy], man." We finally got to Duc Pho and jumped out of the Huey in the high grass close by a firebase. They were pumping out 105s one after another. There was lot of enemy movement. We joined a convoy that was going to take us on this bad road through these hamlets and down to the beach. We were riding in a three-quarter-ton truck near the rear of the convoy. Lieutenant Klempner was standing up in that truck, and instinctively I put a round in the chamber. I clicked off the safety and I laid flat on the floor of the truck.

"What are you doing?" Lt. Klempner asked me.

"Sir, I think you better get down here," I said. "There are no birds."

"What are you talking about?"

"Listen, there are no sounds. This isn't right!" Because you always heard jungle sounds even over the trucks. But this time there was nothing. "Something's not right," I said. "I think something bad is going to happen."

Just then the whole front of the convoy got nailed. They killed the eighteen-year-old boy who was driving. It was awful. They killed him and the lieutenant in the front with him got hit in the arm. They called in air support and nuked both sides of the road with napalm. The sight of burning hamlets and bodies in pieces all along the road was horrible. We finally made it to the beach, where we stayed in an underground bunker overnight. We did what we had to do, and it was time to go back out to the landing zone. It was so dangerous that they had a tank in the front of the convoy, a tank in the back, and a helicopter gunship overhead, or we would have never made it out alive. We got back to base camp and Captain Bon called me in.

"Your orders came in to leave Vietnam on May 29. But I'm going to give you a special order. I want you to go down to Cam Ranh Bay a few days early and just hang around and get out of here, man."

"I appreciate it. I don't think I can do it anymore," I told him. It was sad, because Lieutenant Klempner and I were such good friends. Even though enlisted guys weren't supposed to socialize with the officers, they liked me.

Years later they told me, "We loved you, because we could talk to you about music—you had stuff to say." Lieutenant Klempner volunteered to drive me over to the airbase and we saluted each other. It was tough leaving.

I went down to Cam Ranh and just hung out a couple of days. They had buildings at that point. They had built wooden buildings with the tin roofs and a screen. It felt so nice to sleep on a cot with a warm sheet and a pillow. All I wanted to do was sleep out of the elements and eat decent food. They had a good mess hall there. After two days, sure enough, in came a Northwest Orient jumbo jet and, interestingly, Reed from Conshohocken was on that flight back home. Reed and I came in to Vietnam together and we were going out together. It was May 29, 1967, almost exactly a year from the day we arrived, but it was funny, because in those twelve months I felt like I had lived a dozen lifetimes.

ELEVEN

Back Home—You'd Think I Shot Mickey Mantle

IT WAS A FULL FLIGHT LEAVING VIETNAM, MAYBE 150 GUYS, all ranks and all units. We all sat down, and you could hear a pin drop—not a sound. We started taxiing and as we were picking up speed, instinctively, everybody was holding hands. As we lifted off, most of us had our eyes closed. The pilot came on and said, "If you look out to the left, you'll see your last of Vietnam!" Once we got far out enough over the water and we knew we were out of range, the plane erupted. There were a lot of tears.

We got through all that and flew to Okinawa, then stopped in Tokyo to refuel. Then we flew from Tokyo right to Fort Lewis, Washington. When we landed, Reed was up toward the front of the plane and I was in the back. Guys were standing, and I hollered to him, "Reed."

He said, "I know." So, he waited. Reed and I stepped off the plane onto the ground in America together. We put our feet in Vietnam at the same time and we did the same when we got home. I kissed the ground. We didn't have a phone at home, so there was nowhere to call.

That was probably May 31, 1967, with the time difference and all. My discharge date was supposed to be August 4, but because I had thirty days' leave accumulated, they just let me out of the army at Fort Lewis. Maybe they also took into account that I was on death's door in the field hospitals for over a month and I looked emaciated.

I caught a redeye flight to JFK. That's when I got my first taste of how unpopular I was. Just the looks I got. You'd think I shot Mickey Mantle. It just didn't feel right. I took a taxi into Manhattan to Port Authority. Then I took a bus from Port Authority to Newark. My parents had moved outside of Asbury Park, so I first went to see Aunt Laura and my grandmother. They got in touch with a neighbor who lived in the same building as my parents, who called downstairs to my mother and said, "Billy's home." So my two aunts, Laura and Netty, drove me home from Newark. We pulled up and I got out. I was in my uniform and my mother was at the curb with my brother, Rob, and my sister Patty. She was six.

When I went away, she had just turned five. I remember having her on my knee and just before I left, she said to me, "You're going to come home, aren't you?" I said, "I'm going to do my damnedest." But I couldn't look her in the eye.

I got out of the car and there at the curb I hugged my mother and she had a very concerned look on her face. She said, "Take it easy. Your father isn't well." I didn't know anything about it. My father had had a massive heart attack in March, just before his fifty-third birthday, and he was in the hospital a couple of months. I didn't know it, but the doctor said, "Don't bring your son home," because my father couldn't take the shock of it. I didn't know what it meant. She just said, "Take it easy. Your father's not well."

"Where is he?" I asked.

"Well, he's upstairs and there's a nurse there."

I walked in to find my father, who was a construction guy, a short guy, but a muscular guy reduced to a thin, gray-tone, ashen-looking man with a nurse by his side. I walked over to him and said, "Hi, Dad," and I put my hand out. Here was the guy that probably kissed me last when I was an infant. I don't ever remember him telling me he loved me and never remember him hugging or kissing me. So the nurse helped him to his feet and he turned into this crying, screaming mass of humanity, screaming, "My son, my son." He just kept kissing me and squeezing me, and I didn't know what to do. I didn't know what to make of it. I was completely devastated.

He calmed down a bit and I went in the kitchen and I got a glass of water. My mother was making coffee. The nurse helped my father out of the chair and walked him into the kitchen to sit. Before he sat down, he repeated the whole routine over again. I was completely spent. I was never more confused in my whole life.

Our parents were always broke. My mother's alcoholism and my father's inability to provide properly certainly were major factors, which was why we moved so many times when I was a kid. He was always one step ahead of the landlord. While I was in the army, I arranged to have my money sent home in an allotment to help the best I could. A few months after I got to Vietnam, my brother Richie got his draft notice and was serving in Fort Leonard Wood, Missouri.

One night, the doorbell rang. It was Western Union. Now unless you lived near a base, back then, families would be notified by telegram. They didn't get calls. They got Western Union saying, "We regret to inform you that your son is gone." My sister said that my parents turned ghost white, shaken, like she had never seen anything before. She was six years old at the time. They said, "Go downstairs and get . . ."—the nurse had lived downstairs in the other apartment—"Go down and get Nurse Rowan." My sister said the nurse came up and sat between my parents and opened the Western Union. When my parents were told it was a MoneyGram from my brother in Leonard Wood, she said they both fell on the floor screaming, crying. Then within two mornings, my father had a massive heart attack.

Knowing that, I carried that and worried that someday I would have a heart attack too. Within a week from being home from the war, I was in the emergency room. For years, I was constantly in fear that I was going to have to pay back for my father's illness. Now, I'm home, back in the same dilemma—they had no money, so I was torn. What do I do? It was a terrible situation. My father was sick and now he was disabled. For the first few weeks, I was walking around in my uniform because I didn't know how to be a civilian. I went down to Asbury Park and walked around. I went to Steinbach's Department Store. I walked in and I saw a woman working there whose son I'd known since 1962 hanging on the boardwalk in Bradley Beach. "Hello, Mrs. Hartung," I said. "It's Billy. I'm home."

"I know," she said, and she walked away. Like she didn't want anything to do with me and I knew her quite well for some time before the war. But now I was a soldier, returning from a war that she didn't agree with. I was devastated, and it was happening over and over all over town. Now they just didn't want to deal with me, and I felt so isolated.

I had spent my entire time in Vietnam in remote base camps and wasn't aware of the social changes back home. I was caught completely off guard by the "The Summer of Love" that was in full swing. It was like landing on another planet. I was a fish out of water, having grown up on John Wayne war movies when soldiers were heroes.

So after a few weeks, I took the bus to New York in my uniform. I figured it's only two years and I'll go back to Kama Sutra Records and start over again. But by then they had exploded into a major player in the record business. I walked in and they wouldn't see me. Finally, I got through. I went back after several calls and met with this guy Frankie Mel. Not Artie Ripp or Hy Mizrahi. We met for a few minutes, again in my uniform, and he said, "Well, our roster's strong and there's nothing we can do for you." Here were the people who were grooming me to be the next big thing, who had gone as far as offering me women's bloomers and a dead fish to get out of being drafted. And they barely gave me the time of day. I felt my life was over.

I got on the bus and went back to Asbury Park. When I got off the bus, I glanced over at Jack's Bar down the street. I hesitated at first, but I walked in, which started the downturn. I started drinking. In light of all that, I felt, *Well, I got to do something to help the family.* A few weeks later, I was down in Asbury Park and I stopped in to see an old black fellow that had a shoeshine stand, but he was really a bookmaker. He was a gangster, but his shoeshine stand was the front. He used to book horses and he was a nice guy. I knew him before I went to the war. I stopped in and got a shine and I was talking to him and telling him that the town really changed quite a bit.

"How you doing? How'd you make out?" he asked me.

"Pretty rough, and it's real rough now with the family the way it is."

A businessman came in and sat in the chair next to me and we cracked up a conversation while he was waiting for a shine.

"You're a soldier?" he asked.

"Yes, I just got out. I just came back from Vietnam."

"Well, what are you going to do?"

"Well, I was in the music business before the war, so I'm planning on going back to New York and starting over again." He was kind enough to give me his card.

"Well, if it doesn't work out, soldier," he said, "I own a company down the block. Just come over and I'll find work for you. I'll hire you." I put the card in my pocket. At that point, the family was doing worse and worse and I wasn't getting anywhere, because I was so detached from music, the way music had evolved.

After ninety days of being verbally abused wherever I went for serving my country, naïvely I felt that while it was only two years that I was away, I could go back to work easily in the music business. That obviously wasn't the case. I became a drunk in the street. They were bringing me home dead drunk. I'd walk into bars, bars with these truckers and like a jerk I'd stand there—I was 119 pounds by then—and I'd say, "You want to know something? There isn't a man in this place, there's not. You're not men, you're not men. Anybody here ever serve? Anybody been to war? Anybody? Well, then, you're not a man, don't talk to me."

The owners knew me and felt sorry for me. They'd come over and say, "Billy, for God's sake." My head was just totally screwed up.

I had returned to a country I didn't recognize. Nineteen sixty-eight had seen the country more divided than ever. I felt like dirt and I was being treated like dirt and didn't really understand why.

In his book, *Nixon's White House Wars*, author Patrick J. Buchanan explained what had happened:

The year of Nixon's election, 1968, had seen the nation torn apart by the Tet Offensive, the breaking of President Johnson, the assassinations of Dr. (Martin Luther) King and Bobby Kennedy, the riots that erupted in a hundred cities following King's death, anarchy on campuses, the riotous (Democratic) convention in Chicago, and the war in Vietnam. Half a million US troops were fighting in Southeast Asia, with thirty thousand dead, no end in sight, and caskets coming home every week carrying the remains of two to three hundred of the best and bravest of America's young.

Buchanan went on to point the vast difference in the eight short years between Kennedy's inauguration, January 20, 1961, and Nixon's, January 20, 1969:

By January 20, 1969, we were in another country, no longer one nation and one people, but a land divided by war and race and culture and politics.

After being rejected by Kama Sutra, I decided to open a small office in Asbury Park with a childhood friend of mine, Joe Buxbaum, who had a few bucks to put up. We formed East of Eden Productions, but all we really produced was chaos and the only thing we ever created was a disturbance. It wasn't Joe's fault at all. He was a loyal friend.

I was still totally off the wall and drinking like a complete maniac, so after two months Joe politely said, "Billy, I love you, but this business isn't for me." So I hung on, hardly paid the rent, chased key tenants out of the building with the noise and crazy people I had showing up to audition for me.

I ran an ad in the newspaper calling for talent auditions, not knowing hundreds would show up. It was like backstage at *America's Got Talent*. Incredible! The hallway on the fourth floor outside my office was covered with people practicing what they were going to do for me. The attorney down the hall and the people next door at the advertising agency had to step over comb players, tap dancers, jugglers, organ grinders with monkeys on leashes, hillbilly guitarists, you name it. The building manager on the first floor went ballistic.

The office was so ridiculous. I had no telephone now that Joe left, so I used the phone booth in the lobby. I had an old desk with no chair. I had a towel on the radiator that I sat on, a dirty old couch I picked up out of someone's trash, and an old broken-down piano I bought for twenty-five dollars. One day two FBI agents showed up thinking I was a pornographic company connected with the mafia. They even asked me if I knew Pussy Russo. Then looked at each other as much as to say, "There's no way the mafia would let this guy live, let alone join their club." They just walked out shaking their heads.

A young girl showed up to audition with an acoustic guitar and a water bucket. She walked in, turned the bucket upside down, put one foot on it and started to wail away the worst music at the top of her lungs. The attorney next door beat on the wall so hard I thought it would collapse. He was hollering things I wouldn't say in front of you let alone put in this book. I thought he was going to have a heart attack. I kept beating on the wall back and screaming, "I'm a Vietnam vet, pal, and I'll throw you out the window." Yes, I was a bit crazy too.

Then the best of all was when the shoe salesman from around the corner came in on his lunch break to audition as a nightclub singer. He was dressed in a bright green suit with green socks and shoes. He also wore the worst toupee in history. It looked like he hit it on the highway and it was still clinging to life. He used the metal shoehorn from his job pretending it was a microphone and started singing and doing the horn section arrangements with his mouth in and around the lyrics. I sat there like an oil painting. I couldn't believe it. We remained friends for years. I gave him the nickname "Jimmy Shoes."

Needless to say, after a few months of not paying the rent and chasing many tenants out of the building, I was put in the street. East of Eden went south. I was able to get in the building on a Sunday and took my piano down the street to a bogus antique store that was a front for drug sales and sold it for five dollars so I could buy two drinks. On my way to the store, it was hilarious! I had all the traffic moving slowly behind me pushing the piano about zero miles an hour. People were screaming things at me like, "Give us a song, Sam," and "We're going to take your thumbs, pal." I got the five bucks, went to Jack's Bar, and laughed my ass off.

By late June '68, I was at my lowest point with alcohol. I made a mess of my brother Richie's wedding reception by being the "worst man" not the best man. I was so screwed up. I was drunk at nine o'clock in the morning. I wore clothes that didn't fit me. At the wedding ceremony I was swaying back and forth, trying to get the ring out of my pocket in the church. People wanted to kill me. I was so drunk I passed out and was carried home and put to bed. I must have slept a day and a half.

When I finally woke up, I didn't know where I was at first. I stumbled into the bathroom and laid on the floor hugging the toilet and fell back to sleep. My mother knocked on the door so long she finally walked in and started screaming, thinking I was dead. It was horrible. When I stood up and leaned on the sink, I took a long, hard look in the mirror at someone I could hardly recognize. My skin had a gray tone and my long hair was stuck to my face down to my chin. Staring in the mirror, suddenly a bell went off.

You fool, I thought to myself. *Your mother got her son back and he walked in on his own two legs! You owe it to all those boys who were tagged and bagged to never see another sunrise, so straighten up!* I said, "Son of a bitch, you're going to cut this out and move on, out of respect for all the mothers not as fortunate as yours."

And that was the beginning of the commitment I made to get it together. I continued to let my hair grow long and I just wouldn't tell anybody I was a Vietnam vet. I looked worse than serial killer Charles Manson. I stopped talking about Vietnam completely. Nobody for years knew my legal name, Torsiello, and no one knew I was even in the army, let alone a Vietnam vet. I wasn't going through that again. There was only one guy I talked to about it, for some reason. That was Jim Morrison of The Doors, which I'll get to later.

So, I'm at Jack's one day and I reached in and pulled some money out and the card fell out that the businessman gave me. I picked it up and I said, "You know what? I have to go there." The next morning I went to the office and he hired me. It was a collection agency. I was miserable there, calling people. I was there a few weeks and they had a radio on and it was coming up on lunchtime. I was struggling, because I was calling my relatives. I had to disguise my voice, because I saw that, oops, that's my deadbeat cousin.

Anyway, I was searching for a direction I could relate to on the radio. On one end of the dial were Jimi Hendrix, The Doors, and Jefferson Airplane with the acid rock material. On the other end was The Fifth Dimension with sophisticated chord changes. I felt like a fish out of water. Then one day "Windy" by The Association came on and I thought, *I can do that!* It just stuck with me and drew me back in instantly.

> *Who's peeking out from under a stairway?*
> *Calling a name that's lighter than air?*
> *Who's bending down to give me a rainbow?*
> *Everyone knows it's Windy . . .*

That record ignited something in me. I listened to it, went out to lunch, then I walked up to the bus terminal and got on the bus to New York and I never went back to that office. Although I needed the work, I knew I couldn't do that anymore and I just stopped coming in. I deeply regret never thanking Carl for the job and his kindness, but I've been in the music business ever since. I just went up to New York and roughed it. I slept in the hallways, started paying attention. I found R&B because I couldn't relate to a lot of the music. I bought an old upright piano and I sat there and taught myself how to play it again. I started focusing on R&B and I began writing with my old friend Ray Dahrouge, who was a great inspiration to me.

After nine or ten months meeting almost every morning at my small office at 620 Bangs Avenue in Asbury Park, Ray and I started hitting our stride by concentrating on R&B music. The old upright was out of tune and had a few strings missing but it didn't matter. The music really came from inside of our heads.

We began every morning with coffee and listening to the great songs Kenny Gamble and Leon Huff wrote and produced for Jerry Butler's album, *The Iceman Cometh*. That album included Butler's great anthem, "Only the Strong Survive." We listened to both sides of the album all the way through religiously before going to the piano. Many nights we were still there very late drinking Seagram's Seven and soda, getting blitzed and writing away. We threw all the empty bottles out the window onto a lower roof. After a few months, you couldn't see the roof.

The inspiration for our first hit song, "Never Gonna Let Him Know," undoubtedly came from studying that Butler album. The only problem was I was still drinking, so I slowed down the best I could. After two months I was contributing much more to the music of our songs along with the lyrics. It felt amazing to want to get up and write each day.

Ray was the lead writer, a great writer, but I was pulling up fast. We went back and forth to New York City as much as we could afford to. We knocked on doors at the Brill Building, starting with the top floor working our way down to the lobby of the ten-story building. That's where all the publishers were. The other key building we spent serious time in was 1697 Broadway, four blocks up from the Brill, which was the Ed Sullivan Building at the time, where many small independent music publishers and producers had office space.

One morning we stepped into the elevator and we immediately recognized George Kerr, a very good black producer who we also admired and studied his work. I was always more outgoing than Ray, as he was strictly all about the music. I had moxie and the balance worked well in the long run. It certainly helped open some doors. In the elevator that day, I immediately started a conversation with George.

"You're George Kerr, aren't you? Well, my friend and I have written some great songs we think you'll like." Many years later I met George in the Hard Rock Café building on West 57th Street. He was with singer

Lloyd Price. He told Lloyd that when he was first approached by Ray and me, that he didn't think there was any way in the world we would have anything in his genre but I was so charming he had to at least listen.

We were invited to his office and played a few songs and George was blown away. He immediately invited us back as often as we were in town and ultimately in November '68 he recorded "Never Gonna Let Him Know" with Debbie Taylor at The Hit Factory on West 47th Street, with Jerry Ragovoy engineering. I couldn't believe I was sitting there listening to my first top-five record being recorded. It went on to be number five on the R&B chart, made it to *American Bandstand*, and was all over the radio. I had found a home in R&B and I stayed there. I was living the dream. Thanks to Ray, to be honest. He was driven with a strong sense of urgency that helped keep me in check, as I was happy just being alive. I was enjoying the process with the attitude if it took time, it took time.

By then my father had gotten fed up with me because I had been home for over a year and he felt I wasn't doing much to bring any money home. I was having trouble breaking back into the business. He didn't want to be hard on me, because he had struggled in the music business himself. I guess he also didn't want me to wind up as unhappy as he was. In early '69 he didn't realize that I had stopped drinking too much and that I was on the verge of a hit record. He felt that if he put me out of the house it would be for the best.

"You know what?" he said to me. "Live in your office, do what you want to do, but I can't put up with it anymore here at home." Part of it was that he hated blacks, so he hated that I was playing *that* music in the house and I would have some of *those* people come over. It was a Saturday, and he told me that he wanted me out.

I said, "Okay."

A few weeks had gone by and I knew that "Never Gonna Let Him Know" had been released and was building momentum. I came by the porch on a Saturday to get my stuff and move out.

"Well, if you don't mind," I said to my father, "I want to watch *American Bandstand* before I go, because I'm not going to have a television at the office. I'm going to have to live at that office, so I'd like to see what's going on. If it's okay, I'll just have a coffee."

"All right, go ahead," he said reluctantly. He's sitting there with the pipe, and I already knew that my record was going to be on that show. They used to have a segment called "Rate the Record." They'd play a new record, kids would dance to it, and then they'd have two couples give their opinion. They'd say stuff like, "I give it an 88 because it has a good beat and you can dance to it." They gave our song a 98. The kids said it sounded like Gladys Knight and The Rascals. That was great. So, I'm sitting there and my father's sitting there with the pipe, and now they come to the "Rate the Record" part and it's my record. They're playing the record and he took the pipe out of his mouth, startled.

"Wait a minute. Isn't that your song?" he asked.

"Yes, it's 'Never Gonna Let Him Know,'" I said with a smile. Well, I don't think Neil Simon could have written a better scene. My father was always kind of a hustler. He quickly figured out that I was now a successful songwriter, so switching gears he took the pipe out of his mouth again.

"Bill," he said, "I saw this car and it's only a hundred dollars." It was right out of a scene in Jackie Gleason's *The Honeymooners*, where Gleason's character Ralph was always scheming. I couldn't help but laugh.

"Well, we'd probably work it out, no problem," I said, laughing. Then he went out on the porch and he started carrying my stuff back in.

Ray and I went to BMI. Broadcast Music Incorporated is a performing rights society that collects your royalties for you and keeps track of airplay performances. It was obvious that we had a hit, so they gave us an advance. I think it was a couple thousand bucks, no big deal. I didn't drive so I got a hold of my brother Richie and I said, "Look, I want you to take me down to this place. There's a '61 Dodge that Dad told me about over there." I went and bought it. I told the guy, "Just give me the keys, leave it here, and I'll have my brother bring my father down to pick it up."

I went home, and there was my father sitting on the porch smoking his pipe.

"Here are these keys," I said, handing them to him.

"What's this?" he wanted to know.

"Richie's going to come over and you're going to go get that Dodge. I bought that Dodge for you." It was a great moment, because I was still able to show him some love.

You should have seen the smile on his face.

TWELVE

Traveling with Jimi Hendrix, The Doors, and Cream

THINGS KIND OF ROLLED ALONG FROM THERE. NINETEEN sixty-eight was an interesting year because we were working with a music publisher in the Brill Building, Bob Feldman. He and his partners had written the hit song "My Boyfriend's Back," and they produced The McCoy's number one hit, "Hang On Sloopy." They had become top producers and were now publishing too. One of his partners, Jerry Goldstein, had a company called Poster Ways, and they had the rights for the summer of '68 to manufacture posters of all the big touring rock acts and sell them at the concerts. The artists all got a cut of the royalties.

They were making posters of Janis Joplin, Jimi Hendrix, The Doors, The Chambers Brothers, Soft Machine, Cream, Donovan, and several others. I was the only guy in the operation that didn't do drugs. I had just gotten off the alcohol kick that summer, so I was fairly clearheaded. So they approached me with a proposition.

"How would you like to make some extra money? You can go on a Thursday and take posters to the shows, recruit some buyers, manage the sales, and bring the money back," they said. "We trust you with the money."

It sounded good to me. "Okay," I said, not realizing how historic that tour was going to be.

Jerry and his partner were working out of Feldman's office in the Brill Building, but they rented an apartment at the Westerly on 8th Avenue and 55th Street. They had a large living area, small kitchen, one bath, and two bedrooms. From time to time, though, especially on weekends, people were sleeping everywhere. It was a flophouse in a high rent district. I doubt if Jerry knew half the people that would show up and just stay there for days. He usually went to his bedroom and didn't mingle too much. He was busy and not there during the day very much at all.

His partner was the culprit when it came to inviting people to party all night and ultimately sleep it off, whether on the couch, the floor, or the bathtub. It didn't matter much. They were so out of it, they could've slept in the stairwell and not even realized it. I stayed there a few nights a week between the poster sale dates. I would write with Dahrouge in the office at the Brill and stay at the Westerly until I had to fly out on Wednesday or Thursday. I slept mostly on the floor in a corner of the living space. Sometimes I woke up and there were two naked girls sharing the couch and another stretched out on the floor. It was insane.

All in all, it wasn't terrible. I had an opportunity to stay in the city. I couldn't afford to go back and forth every week anyway, and I was furthering my education—good, bad, or indifferent. The way I saw it, after 'Nam in a bunker all night not knowing if I would see the sunrise, the madness I was witnessing didn't mean anything. Or, as the black boys in 'Nam used to say, "It don't mean nothing!"

It wasn't easy though, sitting there in a circle with people who hated the government and the president and showed no respect for the men and women still stuck in the middle of the war. I had to bite my tongue and suck it up. It wasn't worth getting into it; they were so lost they wouldn't get it anyway, and I didn't want to blow my cover. I blended right in like a super spy and played the game. As in the war, it was all about the objective, and the objective was getting my music career where I wanted it. If this was what it took, so be it.

As luck would have it, I got to travel with some of the artists. The first gigs I attended were with Jimi Hendrix.

Jimi Hendrix played electric guitar like nobody before him or since. In the early '60s he had played backup for some of the greats like Sam Cooke, Jackie Wilson, Little Richard, and The Isley Brothers before heading out on his own, playing a combination of rock, blues, country, R&B, you name it. When Eric Clapton first heard him play in '66, he later described it by saying, "He walked off and my life was never the same again."

By this time, the summer of '68, Jimi was on his way to becoming the highest paid performer in the world. Watching Hendrix was exhilarating, but seeing the lifestyle of all these stars behind the scenes, you knew it couldn't last.

I believe the very first concert I took posters to was in Framingham, Massachusetts. It was an outdoor event. The stage was under a large tent with the audience sitting on the grass. I sold quite a few posters that night before and after the show. That was the first time I watched Jimi play the national anthem with the guitar behind his head. It was incredible. It was also the first time I saw anyone play a guitar made for a right-handed musician played by a left-handed musician upside down. He was tremendous!

It was a weird moment for me. The national anthem always gave me the chills, being very patriotic. Having served in the war made the experience that much more intense. There I was, with a tied-dyed shirt a few sizes too big, stovepipe striped pants, long straggly hair, and mustache. I didn't look like I could've have ever served in the military.

Most of the Hendrix gigs also featured Soft Machine. I never talked to any of the guys, though. They did their thing and I guess went to parties afterward. There was a ton of partying. Another rub for me is that I hated the drug abuse. It was very hard to witness.

When we were in Bridgeport, Connecticut, they were playing the outdoor arena. Before the show began, there was a lot of drama. A guy from Jimi's entourage—it might have been his manager—got into an argument with the local police chief and punched him in the mouth. All hell broke loose.

Several officers showed up and the word was they wanted to take everyone associated with the show downtown. Jimi was in a limo bombed out of his mind and wasn't aware of anything going on. I ran over to the car to give him a heads up. The limo looked like a drug store that had been ransacked. Everything imaginable was scattered on the seat and floor under Jimi's feet. There were several bottles of champagne, as well. Jimi just stared up at me with his eyes opening and closing and never responded. I think it was the promoter of the concert that worked the situation out with the police. We all lucked out and the show was on. It was scary, though, for a very long minute.

Jimi was a very quiet guy. As wild as he was on stage, offstage he was very mellow. Maybe it was his drug use, but at times I felt like there was a little boy inside of him shining through. I didn't realize at that time that he once played with Joey Dee and The Starliters at the Peppermint Lounge on 45th Street in New York City. I was a huge Joey Dee fan in the early '60s when he had the big hit song "Peppermint Twist." I even played the Peppermint Lounge myself one Sunday afternoon when I was part of the Jersey Beatles. Go figure. I wouldn't have recognized Jimi then anyway.

The wildest recollection I have of the Hendrix concerts is when in late August he and Soft Machine were booked at the Rhode Island Arena. It was completely sold out. Thousands and thousands of people showed. Instead of flying there with the posters, I was sent in a station wagon with two other guys from the office. When we got to the arena, there was a ton of commotion and a huge police presence, which was much larger than normal. It was obvious something was wrong. We hung out in the car and waited to get some information before attempting to enter the arena with the posters.

The word was that Jimi didn't show up, and they had no idea if he would show up. The crowd was getting loud and throwing things. The audience in those days showed up stoned out of their minds to begin with and didn't really need much to set them off. We hung out to see if we were on or off. We waited for more than an hour then decided to get out of there before we found ourselves in the middle of a nasty riot. We were convinced that violence was imminent. So, we drove back to the city and arrived in New York around 4:00 a.m. The guys wanted to go to Steve Paul's The Scene on West 46th Street, which was the "in" place back then. It's where photographer Linda Eastman met Paul McCartney. Groups like The Lovin' Spoonful and The Young Rascals used to play there, and no one got in unless Steve Paul okayed it.

When we walked in, I couldn't believe it. Jimi and Mitch Mitchell were on stage playing all night with the house bass player, David Clayton Thomas! This was well before David replaced Al Cooper with Blood, Sweat & Tears and they had their huge hits "Spinning Wheel" and "When I Die." Jimi left thousands of outraged fans out in the cold in Rhode Island, and probably lost huge money, too, to play all night for free at The Scene.

Several years later when I wrote a song and produced it with David Clayton Thomas, we spoke about The Scene and those days with Jimi. David said he and Jimi used to drop acid late at night, get in a boat, and float under the George Washington Bridge with the glowing lights freaking them out. Anyway, that was one crazy night.

The other Rhode Island Arena experience I witnessed was with Cream. The previous night we were at the Baltimore Arena for a show with The Moody Blues. The next day, I got to fly to Rhode Island in a small plane with Jack Bruce and the road crew of Cream. Jack seemed like a levelheaded guy and we chatted a little. I didn't really care for the guys in the crew at all, so I just stayed away from them. I resented how they took advantage of very young girls who would do anything to get close to the stars. As a matter of fact, when we got to Rhode Island the next night, four girls from Baltimore drove all night to get to Rhode Island to the next show. Unbelievable.

One of the girls was only fourteen years old. They were looking to stay with either one of the crew that night or if they were lucky enough, with Eric Clapton or Jack. I didn't witness what ultimately went down. I tried to rescue the youngest girl by offering to let her sleep in my room on the couch. NO STRINGS! She slept a bit but got up a few hours later and slipped out the door without her shoes. I left her shoes outside my door and went back to sleep. The next day one of the guys in the crew got an attitude about me interfering, but I let it go. Frankly, I wanted to split his head open. I had a flashback of the young women who were tormented by the Viet Cong late at night in their mud huts out in the middle of the rice paddies.

The show that night was the final performance by Cream in the U.S. It looked like twenty thousand fans were there all tuned up ready for the time of their lives, and the guys didn't disappoint them. Prior to the show, though, I was in the green room, which was downstairs where the hockey and basketball players would change their clothes and prepare for the games. Jack Bruce and Ginger Baker were down there. I didn't see Eric. As a matter of fact, I only saw Eric when he was on stage.

Ginger Baker was sitting in the corner on a bench with his girlfriend, who had the John Lennon-type round glasses, long curly hair, and a floor-length flowery dress. It was typical for the day. Ginger was ghost white and shaking so bad he was hitting his head on the concrete wall. The girl was holding on to him as tight as she could to keep him from hurting himself. When Jack came in, I said, "Jack, how in the world is Ginger going to play this show?"

He said, "You'll see." And he was right.

Terry Reid, a British rocker, was the opening act and was very good. I hung out with him after the show and we played a few of our songs for each other. Very cool guy. He was intrigued with Brill Building stories, and I had 'em. Shortly after Terry finished his set, they announced Cream. The applause was so deafening, I thought the building would collapse. It was amazing.

The guys played an incredible set and killed the crowd with every song. As they approached the end of the show, Eric and Jack walked off stage, and Ginger did a drum solo that went on for almost thirty minutes. Two kick drums, I believe two snare drums, and a ton of tom toms roaring like a pack of lions. He played the kick drums like lightning, rumbling a hundred miles an hour, making the rafters shake. I was stunned and totally in awe of how he could get through it. Finally, Eric and Jack came back out on stage with cans of shaving cream and began to cover Ginger from head to toe. The thing that killed me was that he continued to play the solo and never missed a beat. It was like he was possessed.

After three or four encores the show was over. Once again, I had no idea the history I had witnessed. I went back down to the green room to bring up more posters and there was Ginger and his girlfriend sitting in the same place. Again, he was shaking like a leaf, ghost white, hitting the wall again. It was one of strangest experiences I witnessed that summer on the road with all those icons.

There were fun moments on the road I did enjoy. I needed an occasional break from watching such brilliant talent destroy themselves night after night. I worked one Donovan concert in Philadelphia. His father was a total trip. Sweet, sweet guy. I really liked him. He would stand outside the venues with photos of his son for sale. He even had Donovan buttons on his suspenders holding up his pants and on his straw hat. Hilarious! He was one of the proudest dads in the world, though. For me, that evening was a welcome break from the madness. Donavan's audience was more subdued as the music and performance was intimate and relaxing.

What was most depressing was going back to New York on Mondays to turn in the cash and receipts from the poster sales. Jerry Goldstein had a partner who was a maniac. The partner thought he was cool ordering me around like a flunky to go get coffee and bagels, then sitting there dropping acid in the coffee and drinking it like it was just another day at the office.

If I had to pick the most difficult thing about the six or eight weeks I toured with all those acts, it would have to be the audience—all bombed out of their minds and extremely rude. I remember being offered all kinds of drugs in exchange for a free poster and when I refused, they became incredibly abusive. I was even offered sex for a poster one evening. A young girl, probably no more than fifteen or sixteen, was so out of her mind, I doubt if she even knew what she was saying. Either way, I wasn't doing it!

This photo was taken in Bridgeport, Connecticut, in August 1968 at a Jimi Hendrix and Soft Machine concert fourteen months after I came home from the war.

August of '68 was a very hot and humid month. One night it was so bad, it was unbearable. My feet were in terrible shape with jungle rot from 'Nam. I had to apply ointment the VA gave me and could only wear white socks. Anything other than white would cause my feet to swell to a point where I could hardly walk. My hippie appearance helped me blend right in with the crowd. The hair, raggedy mustache, the flowered shirt two or three sizes too big, the stovepipe bell-bottom pants, and sandals. I looked just like they did, with one exception—my white socks. I was sickened by how many so called "Do-your-own-thing, everything-is-beautiful, out-of-their-mind idiots" felt compelled to go out of their way to ridicule and embarrass me with homophobic, profane insults for wearing white socks with sandals.

I couldn't help thinking back a few short years before going to 'Nam, when I looked like Frankie Avalon and was writing fun pop songs on guitar with three or four chords for groups like The Duprees. I thought back to those days, then said to myself, *What the hell am I doing standing in the middle of a crystal-blue, smoke-filled field on "the other side of rock and roll"?*

I never had much of a chance to hobnob with the stars. I talked to Hendrix when you could talk to him, when he was relatively coherent. I never really got a chance to talk to Clapton. He was always off by himself, and Ginger Baker, the drummer who founded Cream, was out of his mind.

I spoke to Hendrix I think twice. Once at the Singer Bowl on Long Island in August 1968. I wasn't working on that one. I accompanied Bob Feldman to the huge concert. Jimi broke a guitar strap during his performance and left it on the stage. I picked it up and kind of waved to him with it.

"Cool," he nodded to me. He obviously didn't mind if I kept it. Then the sweetest young blond girl walked up to me without saying a word and kissed me on the cheek. I gave her the guitar strap and never said a word and walked away. I can only imagine what that strap would be worth today!

———————

One Doors concert was in Milwaukee, Wisconsin, at the arena out there. I flew in and got set up. I was staying in the same hotel and saw an incredible show. The next day, I was up, out at the airport, and ready to get a flight back to New York. Jim Morrison was another interesting guy. He was lead singer of The Doors and was known for his poetic lyrics and unique singing style. They hit it big the year before when "Light My Fire" went to number one, and of course Ed Sullivan wanted them for his show. They agreed to come on that September of 1967, but Sullivan wanted Morrison to promise *not* to sing the word "higher" in the line "*Girl, we couldn't get much higher.*" Morrison agreed but sang it anyway, and Sullivan was furious. The producer threatened to ban the group from ever doing the show again. "That's all right," said Morrison. "We just did the Sullivan show."

Anyway, I was in the coffee shop at the airport when Morrison and I got to talking. For some strange reason, as whacked out as Morrison was on stage, to talk to him, he was like a child. He was easy going and a very bright guy.

"What else are you doing for these guys?" Morrison asked me in a soft-spoken kind of way.

"I'm doing the poster thing here, but I'm also writing," I said, kind of surprised at how easy it was to talk to him. "I was signed to Kama Sutra, and then I got a draft notice and had to go to Vietnam, got back, and started over again." For some reason, I felt comfortable doing that with Jim.

"Really?" he said. "That must have been a hoot."

"It was a pretty rough time, but to be honest with you, it's pretty rough readjusting, as well. So much has changed since '65. But I'm in for the long haul and doing the best I can." We talked a bit, but Jim was the only guy I kind of felt comfortable telling that part of my life to. Then, he had to catch another plane.

It was clear very early on that what I was witnessing was a disaster waiting to happen with these rock stars. Prior to going out with the posters, I was invited to the concert I mentioned earlier at the Singer Bowl in Flushing Meadows–Corona Park in Queens, New York. The show was incredible. All on one bill were Jimi Hendrix, Janis Joplin, Big Brother and the Holding Company, Soft Machine, and The Chambers Brothers. There were so many people smoking pot, the police could've simply declared the venue a prison, locked the gates, and left it at that. The most shocking thing was when it was time for Janis Joplin to perform.

On the way to the stage, Janis cracked open a fifth of Southern Comfort and began taking big gulps immediately. All through her set she took big swigs from the bottle. But, as with Ginger Baker in Rhode Island, she never missed a note or a beat. By the end of her set, she dropped the empty bottle on the stage and staggered off. The band just seemed to round up their gear and put it in the VW bus out back like nothing happened. Janis was stretched out with her legs hanging over the back fender, but the guys just worked around her. I guess it was business as usual.

As I did with Jimi's broken guitar strap, I picked up Janis' empty Southern Comfort bottle. But I threw it in the trash. I often wonder if that might have been another missed "golden opportunity" to cash in. I had no idea at the time I was right in the middle of an amazing history unfolding before my eyes. I was more like a fly behind the wall as opposed to on the wall. I just didn't get it. If I had, I certainly would've gotten every poster I was selling signed by the stars. Today they would probably fetch over $100K. Who knew?

In any event, toward the end of the poster sales tour in late September, Ray and I were writing one night when he asked me how things went out there on the road. "It had to be a learning experience, right?" he said.

"Well, I did learn one thing," I told him. "It will be a miracle if Jimi, Janis, and Jim ever see their fortieth birthdays." Sadly, I was right. They all died sad, tragic deaths—all three at the age of twenty-seven!

The writing's on the wall
and, though many of the adjectives are unprintable,
basically what it says there is that
"BABY NOW THERE'S TWO OF YOU"MMS-126
by **TERRELL & DAHROUGE**
on ⊌METROMEDIA RECORDS
is HEAVY

METROMEDIA RECORDS, 3 — 54TH STREET, NEW YORK, N.Y. 10022

The full page ad in *Cash Box* magazine that literally destroyed our career as R&B artists.

THIRTEEN

Terrell and Dahrouge: Two White Guys Singing R&B

I'VE OFTEN BEEN ASKED IF MY OWN VIEWS TOWARDS the war changed at all. I think the honest answer is, for the first few years, especially the first year, I was so bombed out of my head that I rarely thought about it. The exception would have been if I made a mistake and was in the room when the newscast was on, and then I'd go out of my mind. It made me sick. If I saw familiar images of casualties covered with ponchos or flag-draped coffins arriving at Dover Airbase in Delaware, it put me in such a tormented state of mind I would sit in the dark for hours. I realize now that I was suffering from survivor's guilt. A horrible feeling of helplessness.

It wasn't until the spring of '68 after the Tet Offensive, when I was at my low point, that I started opening my mind up to it. Then, I saw lots of different viewpoints. I resented the antiwar demonstrations. However, I was aware that there was a core group that really believed what they were opposing. They really believed it. It was their conviction that they were against this. I didn't agree, but they were committed. It was honest, whether I liked it or not.

What I really resented was the craziness of the people who seemed to just show up because it was the "in" thing to do. It felt very similar to watching many of the people who went to concerts. With all the screaming that goes on at a concert, I don't know how anybody can really enjoy it. They do, but I mean, it's not all about the music—it's about the moment. It's about being there. It's about being part of something. That's the feeling that I got from a lot of the demonstrations, especially in New York. I understood the sentiment of people that were truly sincere. Maybe they had lost friends or members of their family or they came out of an educational institution which put it all in their head from their viewpoint, because educators were planting a lot of negative seeds.

But I did realize, also, when it came to me, that a lot of these people were just there as troublemakers. They were not the ones really trying to get a change going and to make a point. These were the knuckleheads that were throwing the cold water on the whole thing. That was a struggle for me, because now you're double insulting me. You're not only insulting me by rubbing in my face that my service didn't matter and that I shouldn't have done it, but now you're rubbing in my face that you're a knucklehead and you're just part of a movement and it's not really a conviction.

You're there just to join in because that's a place to smoke pot and act like an idiot. That was a double whammy for me, and it bothered me a lot. Then I realized the busier I got, the better off I was. I buried myself in my work. Ray and I were writing up a storm and soon started putting songs on the charts. For me, the process was the magic. I enjoyed the music, but the *life* was the reward. Every song, every record, every moment.

The more we wrote together and sang the demos together of the songs we wrote, the more the team of Terrell and Dahrouge got into a groove. We sounded damn good together and for a while it looked like we were about to hit it big as R&B recording artists too. We were the forerunner of Hall & Oates. Daryl Hall and John Oates were two white guys from Philly who sang soul and R&B. They came along a few years after us and made it big.

The R&B stations loved the songs we were writing, but we ran into a big snag as artists. We were recording and writing under our names, Terrell and Dahrouge, and Terrell sounded like a black name. Think Tammi Terrell. Our music was amazingly received on radio. We put records on the charts and the stations played our music, and then both Capitol and Metromedia Records wanted to sign us.

Around October of '68, Gary Kannon (Katz as he is known now for his work with Steely Dan in the '70s) joined Bob Feldman at the Greenlight office in the Brill. They started producing together. As the Terrell and Dahrouge songs were getting stronger and stronger, they decided to reach out to labels to sign us. In early '69, Bob and Gary first approached Artie Kornfeld at Capitol Records. At this point in his career, Kornfeld was a very successful songwriter and producer. He co-wrote "Dead Man's Curve" for Jan and Dean and wrote the classic "The Rain, the Park & Other Things" for The Cowsills. Later that year, in the summer of '69, he became world famous as the creator and promoter of Woodstock.

Ray and I waited in the lobby while Bob and Gary spoke with Artie. About thirty minutes later, the guys came out with Artie. At that point, Kornfeld stuck out his hand.

"Welcome to Capitol Records," he said, smiling. We were amazed.

"What songs did you like best?" we wanted to know.

"Bob and Gary are my ears," he said. "If they like it, I like it."

Unbelievable! We were ecstatic, to say the least. We went back to Asbury and before long, the word was all over town. Terrell and Dahrouge were signing with Capitol Records. A lot of jealousy was running rampant from the other musicians in town who felt they were much more deserving of the opportunity. That included several who were starting out at the

Upstage, where Springsteen was still in his teens playing there.

As we were waiting for contracts from Capitol, Feldman and Kannon told us that they wanted us to meet with Metromedia, a new label just getting started and hadn't signed any acts yet. We had recently recorded a few piano/vocal demos at Dick Charles Studios on 7th Avenue, so we took the acetates to the meeting. The three songs were: "You Better Look Around," a light, catchy pop tune that me, Ray, and our friend Ebbie Woolley wrote; "Watching the Children," a great song Ray wrote about black and white children holding hands in the schoolyard; and "Simple Black and White," a song Ray and Ebbie wrote which was right on the money also for the social climate of the day.

We met with Len Levy, president of the label, and his vice president, Manny Kellem, at the offices at 1500 Broadway across from the Ed Sullivan building. They listened to all three acetate disks. Within seconds, they said, "We're in!" We were happy to hear that they liked what we did and were appreciative, but we were more excited about the Capitol opportunity. Without consulting with us, Feldman and Kannon turned down the Capitol offer and took the Metromedia deal. Their thinking was: Metromedia being a new label, we would get more attention than going up against a solid roster like Capitol had. We went along with it, and Ray even came up with an excellent new song called "Baby Now There's Two of You" that we recorded a few months later.

It wasn't until June '69 that our first single was released. I felt that "Watching the Children" was the perfect vehicle since our names were well known at R&B radio and the message was right on the money. Our producers and the label decided to run with "Baby Now There's Two of You," which was a great song and sounded a lot like where Hall and Oates would settle in the '70s. I personally thought it was a mistake to come out with that as our first record. We had an R&B base, so why not start there and come back with the pop song and cross over?

The first weekend that the record came out, it was the most played record from New York to Atlanta on every R&B station. *Billboard* magazine did a review. They predicted we would win a Grammy. The record company called the producer, and the producer called us up on a Sunday night. We had sold two thousand records the first weekend in Philadelphia.

They sent product down to Universal Distributors on Thursday, and they went through the records at retail—actual customers—in three days. The record was on the radio less than a week, on all three R&B stations in that market. You couldn't find a copy in the stores. They hauled us up to New York and they hired a rock photographer, Benno Friedman, to shoot us. Oh, God, they followed us around New York all day. He took pictures of Terrell and Dahrouge sitting on a park bench, all these different pictures. They took one with graffiti on the wall.

Our record was the third release on the newly formed Metromedia Records in June 1969.

METROMEDIA RECORDS NEW RELEASE

TERRELL AND DAHROUGE

"BABY NOW THERE'S TWO OF YOU"

"I'M HAPPY MAKING YOU HAPPY"

MMS - 126

It's generally agreed that the successful young recording artist today must write his own material. It's too difficult to get into "someone else's head," and attempt to offer musical suggestions to the new breed of entertainer.

Such is the case with Billy Terrell and Ray Dahrouge. Here are two young men from New Jersey who have found compatibility in their writing and in their performance. They write very "commercially," and we feel they're about to become a very important part of our business.

Samples Ship: 6/4/69

ADV-ML, PRO, SLS, MOS, PA

Our promotion sheet put out by Metromedia Records to announce our first record release.

The following week, when *Cash Box* magazine came out, we had a full page ad that said: "Some of the words on this wall are unprintable, but the message is simple, that Baby, Now There's Two of You, by Terrell and Dahrouge, is heavy."

We were where Hall & Oates leveled off a few years later. We never heard of them back then, but we were like Daryl Hall and John Oates, two guys from Jersey who also loved to sing R&B. Even our beat and everything was like Hall & Oates.

The magazine comes out, and now we're preparing to do the album because the record's going like a house on fire. Len Levy, the president of the company, sent us a message to come to the office as soon as possible.

"I don't know how to tell you gentlemen this," he said. "But we just got word that we have to cancel your album deal."

"What?" I said.

"We can't invest in the album."

"Well, the record is flying."

"No," he said, "you don't understand. Our promotion men called from the field and every station playing your record dropped it. Once they saw that you were white, you were done."

There was one DJ that opened his show on a Sunday morning and apologized to his audience and he let them hear him smash our record in a million pieces on the desk. That was painful! It ruined Terrell and Dahrouge, because we were writing great songs. Our first release should've been "Watching the Children," which was a song about unifying little white hands and black hands forming a circle in a schoolyard. One of the lines was, "They have a grip that's so strong, if they can learn to hang on, a whole lot of things have to change."

We were ahead of all of them with that message. Those stations weren't ready for white guys to sing R&B, which Hall & Oates proved could be done. Metromedia shouldn't have given up on us so easily. Everyone loved the records. Look, for a long time, folks thought The Righteous Brothers were black. They got their name in '63 when they were singing at a marine base in Irvine, California, and some black marines kept saying, "You're righteous, brothers!" They also had the advantage of having Barry Mann write songs for them like "You've Lost That Lovin' Feelin'" and the great Phil Spector arrange and produce it.

It could have happened for us with the right management. Especially with a song like "Simple Black and White" which just laid it out there, that "Enough is enough, let's get with the music." The song had a similar lyric to "Ebony and Ivory," the 1982 recording by Paul McCartney and Stevie Wonder. But they insisted on "Baby Now There's Two of You" because it had a pop beat and melody. It was a great record!

We got out of the deal and it just took the wind out of our sails. We went over to Paramount Records. Ray had written two pop songs that sounded very white and very commercial. We sat at the piano for Jack Weideman, the vice president of Paramount Records in the Gulf & Western Building in Columbus Circle. We played the two songs live, and he said, "Welcome to Paramount."

We were so distraught that we decided that we wanted to produce our own records, which was a big mistake, because we hadn't come along enough in the business yet. Nevertheless, we insisted on being in control of our music going forward after what we had experienced at Metromedia. We switched gears and began writing poppy songs, which was another mistake. After two single releases, we were getting a lot of "pop" airplay, and then the company wanted to do an album even though we didn't have a hit yet. We had a lot of airplay, because I was a good salesman out there on the road.

The first record on Paramount was "You Got to Me, Stephanie." It was a bubble-gummy song. It was like something the Partridge Family would do, but here we were, two R&B guys. It wasn't us. We were writing our best. Some of our strongest songs were almost like southern R&B gospel songs, those R&B ballads. We were kings of R&B ballads with lyric ideas like "He Knows My Key (Will Always Be In The Mailbox)." But now, we found ourselves writing like we were The Monkees or something. It made no sense, and it was getting to us.

The second record was more pop/country, a little more middle-of-the-road. Both the A- and B-sides, "I Really Touched You Once Upon A Time" and "I'll Always Want To See You One More Time," were real good songs, and both started to get airplay. The company called us in with a plan in mind.

"Look, we're getting some traction, so why don't we do an album, and then we can justify putting money into this. We can sell albums for a lot more than we can sell these singles."

I didn't think we should come out with an album before we had a hit.

"No," I said adamantly. "I don't think we should do the album."

It was one of those times I look back on and realize it was probably a mistake, but at the time, I thought to myself, *You know what? We're going to do all this and it's not Terrell and Dahrouge. That's not what we do.* Plus, we weren't prepared to go on the road as an act to promote an album. At that point, we weren't getting along very well either. Ray was under lot of pressure. He and his wife had two children and another on the way. It was best to just go back to writing songs for other artists, which we did.

In the spring of 1970, I sweet-talked my way back into my rundown office at 620 Bangs Avenue in Asbury Park based on the deals Terrell and Dahrouge had as producers.

We had five records placed with five different record labels, and one by one they failed, for a variety of reasons.

Once again things were so tight I couldn't pay the rent for months. The building manager was so mad he turned off the lights and heat to try and force us out. Finally, he came up one day with an ultimatum.

"That's it," he said. "The owners want me to have the police cart you away."

I made a plea telling him we had one more record coming out so all we needed was another month.

"What record?" he asked, suspiciously. Dahrouge had written a whacky novelty song that Musicor Records thought was worth taking a shot with.

"'A Smart Monkey Doesn't Monkey with Another Monkey's Monkey,'" I said, straight-faced.

He stared at me for about twenty seconds and then went ballistic.

"If you don't vacate the premises by five o'clock, I'll have you dragged out."

So, we left. Believe it or not, the record came out a few weeks later. The label called and said, "Read Earl Wilson's column today." Earl Wilson was a nationally syndicated entertainment writer whose column, It Happened Last Night, was read coast to coast.

"The going bananas song title sweepstakes this week," Earl wrote, "has to go to 'A Smart Monkey Doesn't Monkey with Another Monkey's Monkey'!!!"

I bought an extra copy and sent it to the building manager with a note that said, "Earl Wilson gets it, Dick Head!"

But Ray and I had run our course. He went and signed with Cashman & West, a hot songwriting and producing team who discovered and were producing the late, great Jim Croce. I moved on as an independent writer/producer. I caught on in the mid-'70s as a producer and I've been doing it ever since.

By 1973 I was performing, writing, and beginning to get traction as a producer.

FOURTEEN

Rebooting Frankie Avalon's Career

SO, IT'S BEEN A GOOD RUN. I'VE DONE OVER TWO THOUSAND records. I've had sixty-two on the national and international charts, including *Larry Carlton Plays The Sound of Philadelphia: A Tribute to Kenny Gamble & Leon Huff* in 2010, which held chart positions for nearly an entire year.

In 1959 I loved the song "Venus" by Frankie Avalon when I was in eighth grade. I loved it. Matter of fact, in my autograph book, when I graduated eighth grade there was a page of my favorites. My favorite actor was Lloyd Bridges because I liked that show *Sea Hunt.* My favorite book was *Shadow in the Pines,* and I wrote in there that my favorite song was "Venus" by Frankie Avalon, 1959.

In the mid '70s, after Terrell and Dahrouge ended, I was writing and producing for De-Lite Records on an independent basis. I had a great relationship with Freddie Vee, who initially was just an investor in the company but took it over with his son. These were tough fellas but a lot of fun to hang with, most of the time. They were connected guys, but they're all gone now, so there's no harm in mentioning it. There was a lot of underworld money in the music business back then, especially with smaller independent labels. You had to deal with them, because those are the companies that were giving you the shots. You had to start somewhere. I wasn't involved in any illegal activity, but I knew it went on. I just kept my mouth shut and made my music.

One day in early October of '75, I got a call from Freddie. "Billy," he said, "some friends of ours asked us to help Frankie Avalon." At that time, Frankie's recording career was at a low point. "We want to know what we should do from your perspective." Except, he didn't use words like perspective, by the way.

"We want to know what you want to do."

I said, "Sign him." They thought I'd say no, because they were ready to go back and say, "We talked to our producer and he can't do anything."

"What do you mean?" he asked.

"Sign him," I repeated. "You asked me—I would sign him."

"What the hell are you going to do?"

"I'll figure it out," I said. "Let's have a meeting with him and, if he likes it, I would sign him."

The initial meeting with Avalon was at De-Lite Records, located at 200 West 57th Street on the eleventh floor. After getting acquainted, we moved on to what we should have him record. Frankie brought in a demo of a song a friend of his in Texas wrote called "Thank You for That Extra Sunrise," which was along the lines of something Bobby Vinton might record, like "My Melody of Love." I wasn't crazy about it. It was like a polka beat and I'm saying to myself, "What am I going to do with that?" But I kept quiet.

I got on the piano and played and sang "Somewhere Over Arizona," which the label already loved since I had co-written the song with my friend Ebbie a few months earlier. Frankie loved the song, as well, and everyone in the room agreed to move forward with a session. Then I said, "I have a suggestion."

A few months before, I had stumbled onto this disco beat that people were dancing to. I couldn't get it out of my head. I came up with a disco arrangement in my head of "Venus."

They were all ears until I suggested a remake of Frankie's biggest hit, "Venus," back in 1959 with the new up and coming disco beat. Frankie really didn't want to touch the song. The record label resisted the idea because the publishing rights weren't available.

Then, I suggested allowing me to have the musicians play my arrangement of "Venus" as the last song on the date and not spend more than ten minutes of studio time. Joe Renzetti was the official arranger who did a marvelous job orchestrating what I heard in my head. We did two takes and the magic was there without question. When Frankie came to Philadelphia on the 15th of November 1975 to record and heard the track, he was amazed. He did a great job. We finished the single right away, and De-Lite rushed it out before the end of the year.

The *Venus* album released in 1976 after the disco single took off on the charts.

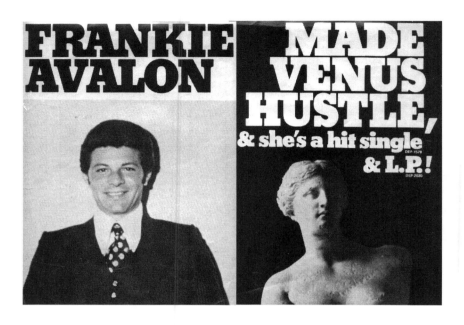

The De-Lite Records promotional poster for in-store placement.

Frankie's De-Lite Records promo photo in 1975.

"Frankie's career had tapered off," I told Charlene Chamberlain in a local TV interview a few years ago. "Paul Anka had written ten songs and did demos especially for Frankie and went around trying to sell him but was turned down by fourteen different labels. That October, Frankie was ready to sign an agreement to play five nights a week in the lounge of a hotel in Hawaii. I said, 'With all due respect, Frankie, I think our only chance is to capture this new beat they're calling disco.' He put his voice to it and a few weeks later we were on the charts."

The record went to number one on the Billboard Adult Contemporary chart in less than a month, and we were off to the races. We were huge on the disco charts and in clubs across the country. Our record inspired several classic artists from the '50s and '60s to do disco versions of their popular songs. Overnight, Frankie was back on top again. All in one week, he was on *The Dinah Shore Show*, *The Mike Douglas Show*, *The Merv Griffin Show*, *The Midnight Special*, *American Bandstand*, and *The Sonny & Cher Comedy Hour*. Then, the big payoff came to the table.

It was a phenomenon. That's what attracted movie producer Allan Carr to put Frankie in the 1978 movie *Grease* as Teen Angel, singing the now iconic tune "Beauty School Drop-Out." And he's never looked back.

To this day, I often look back to those days and my association with De-Lite Records with great affection. I began pitching material to De-Lite in 1971, four years before the Avalon opportunity. I was pounding the pavement up and down Broadway, pitching my songs to any company that would give me a listen. The door was always open at De-Lite. I could depend on getting a listen and a few hundred bucks advance if Freddie liked what he heard. Always in cash. That's the way it was. Far more courtesy than I was afforded at most of the major labels.

De-Lite Records was unconventional, to say the least. I once placed a master recording there for a $1,500 advance. We signed off on the agreement, and a moment later, Freddie moved a file cabinet and pulled up a corner of the carpet to get the money for me. Unbelievable! I used to joke around a lot during the studio sessions. "Hey guys, we're doing this record today for De-Lite Records, the music you can't refuse!" The musicians loved it. Big fun!

Back in the day, it was common knowledge that cash was king when it came to getting airplay on R&B stations. Prior to Freddie and his cousin Fred, the acting president of De-Lite, taking over the day-to-day operations, airplay was marginal. The first thing they did was bring Stan Price on board, a black promotion man from Neptune, New Jersey. Stan was a very likeable man. I liked him a lot. Freddie took Stan on the road with a briefcase full of hundred dollar bills and visited stations from New York to Charlotte. When they were leaving one of the stations, Fred noticed an elderly black man mopping the floor.

"Stanley, pay the guy," Fred said.

"Fred," said Stan quizzically, "the guy's a janitor."

Fred was half serious when he responded, "They might make him a disk jockey some day!"

All in all, Freddie and I became good friends. Many afternoons we would hang out at the China Pavilion, a restaurant and bar on the ground floor of De-Lite's office building. We would drink scotch, eat egg rolls, and talk about a lot of stuff. Not all music related. Sometimes, after several drinks, he would confide in me about things I made sure I forgot the minute we left the bar.

Even though De-Lite was a black music label, prior to bringing Frankie Avalon on board, Freddie had two other white artists he was looking after for some friends: Jeanne Napoli and Jimmy Angel. They were marginal talents, but it didn't matter. Their music was a moot point. They were there under the protection of Freddie Vee. In the spring of 1975, I signed Benny Troy to the label, a soulful white artist, and De-Lite released "Feel the Need in Me" by Genya Ravan. But De-Lite knew that R&B and soul was where they made their money. And with groups under contract like Kool & the Gang, Crown Heights Affair. and The Kay-Gees, they didn't miss a meal.

Many in the industry looked down on De-Lite back then, but thanks to Freddie Vee, Avalon's recording career was rejuvenated and I became an established record producer worldwide. From there, my career as a producer took off. I kept making disco records. I wrote and produced "Rio de Janeiro," which is considered one of the iconic underground songs of the genre, still being played all over Europe. My music is much more popular in Europe—England, France, Germany—than it is here, although the jazz recordings I've produced over the last decade have all charted.

FIFTEEN

Producing the Great Helen Reddy and Bobby Rydell

AROUND 1985 I WAS HIRED BY MOSES KATZ AT MASTERED Records in Mexico to produce an album with Jessica Williams, who had a huge disco run with songs like "Queen of Hearts." Jessica was well known worldwide as a disco diva in the heyday. We got a lot of attention in the clubs in many territories with my song "Limelight." At that time, Jessica was working as a backup singer for Helen Reddy on the road. Helen agreed to sing a duet with Jessica on the album and I was thrilled to have a chance to work with her.

When I met Helen for the first time in L.A., we hit it off very well. She was comfortable working with me. She was participating in a duet with Jessica on a song written by Pam Tillis, the late Mel Tillis' daughter, called "Mysterious Kind." I was surprised when Helen went out in the studio, got on the microphone, and before she started singing, she called to me and said, "Billy, come out here and stand next to me while I do this." She put her arm around me the whole time she was singing, and we got it in two takes.

I didn't feel compelled to approach her for future opportunities at that point, being she was doing us a huge favor. But that was the beginning of a very nice rapport with Helen for years to come. I kept an eye out for opportunities to take to Helen with hopes eventually we would do a project together.

I went back to Helen few years later and told her I had funding for a Christmas album, knowing she had never done one before. She turned it down, explaining she had converted to Judaism after marrying Jeff Wald, her second husband. I understood but persisted in my quest for an acceptable concept, knowing Helen was so right for another hit project.

In 1991 shortly after the success of Tony Bennett and Harry Connick Jr., I saw the writing on the wall that the *The Great American Songbook* was beginning to resonate with a whole new audience. I reached back out to Helen Reddy and suggested we consider doing a tribute project to Sammy Cahn, who co-wrote most of Frank Sinatra's biggest hit songs, along with many other classics in *The Great American Songbook*.

Helen Reddy has one of the most gorgeous voices I have ever heard, and she has an incredible talent to put a song over. After winning a singing contest, the Australian-born Reddy came to America with her three-year-old daughter, Traci, in tow, seeking a career. Down to her last twelve dollars, she met her husband Jeff Wald, who worked at the William Morris Agency. It took a while, but Wald eventually got Reddy an opportunity at Capitol Records where she scored with "I Don't Know How to Love Him" in 1972. She followed that up with her anthem, "I Am Woman," which she co-wrote, and she was off to the races. "I Am Woman" was one of three number one songs she had in '70s on the Billboard Hot 100, along with "Delta Dawn" and "Angie Baby." The fact that she reached number one eight different times on Billboard's Adult Contemporary charts made her, in my mind, a perfect fit for *The Great American Songbook*.

Then I went to Helen with the idea. I explained that with the recent success of Natalie Cole's duet with her dad, Tony Bennett's simple *Steppin' Out* CD, and the rising star Harry Connick Jr. all doing standards, she would be a perfect fit for a new generation of listeners. My idea was to have her record a tribute to Sammy Cahn called *I've Heard That Song Before* with a double CD package that I felt would work very well as a direct response piece on television. Prior to mentioning it to Helen, I met with Sammy and he loved it and agreed to be in the video spot with Helen.

At first, Helen was all ears, asking about what songs I think we should focus on, how many musicians we should have on the project, and what I thought our odds were to be successful. I explained everything in detail. At first, I felt confident that she got it and would agree to move forward. However, for whatever reason, which I still don't understand, Helen turned it down. I was very surprised, but I respected her so much I just let it go.

I was 0 for 2 with Helen at that point but I never gave up hope that one day she would agree to do a project with me. In 1998 another opportunity came up when I pitched a concept to a new label, Touchwood Records. I pitched a tribute project to honor women who made substantial contributions to *The Great American Songbook,* featuring Helen Reddy. I caught up with Helen through a mutual friend and I explained that I had a company interested in meeting with us and discussing my concept. Helen had quite a few questions. We spoke for the better part of an hour.

I made the case that she was the perfect artist to pay tribute to successful women in show business, having sung the pro-women anthem "I Am Woman." Interestingly, Helen wasn't fond of being stigmatized as "Ms. Reddy." I found that out after I first met her and wrote letters addressed to Ms. Helen Reddy. She would say, "That's not necessary, I'm Helen."

I went on to explain the concept would be a CD/DVD package of songs written and/or performed by iconic female stars through the years, along with an on-camera short documentary of the history of women in music. I believed the concept was perfect for direct response television sales. We could reach her core audience right in their living rooms in prime time and all they had to do is pick up the phone and order the package. We wouldn't have to deal with any major record labels and play that game with little reward at the end of the day. That got Helen's attention and she agreed to take the meeting with the Touchwood people.

A few months later she was booked for a week at the Rainbow Room in New York City. The day before she opened, we had our meeting and we were a go. The company loved the project and they were encouraged to know that my partner, Joe Tarsia, and I had been doing a very nice business at QVC since 1996. The door and checkbook were open. I was thrilled.

My wife and I attended opening night at the Rainbow Room and were happy to see the turn out. Helen and I spoke earlier that day about the Touchwood project and she was up for it all the way. I thought she would be really pumped up when it came to show time. After she opened with a few songs, she greeted the audience and made the playful point, "No, I'm not Anne Murray." Helen was often mistaken for Anne Murray, who sang in a similar style.

I thought it was going very well when, out of the blue between songs, some fans started getting impatient for her hits and started calling out for certain songs. When she was called out, she said, "Piss off, I'll get to them when I want to." Helen was known for saying piss off, which was much more commonly used in Australia or the U.K. Instantly, it felt like there was a dark cloud over the whole room.

I couldn't believe it. I knew there were writers there covering her for the morning papers. I sat back and said to myself, "What the hell is she doing?"

Sure enough, I get a call the next day from Irv Beigel, the VP at the label, saying that Lisa Schiff, the Founder/President of Touchwood, saw the reviews and said, "Kill the deal!" We had $150K on the table and it all went away after one performance. Helen sunk the ship. What was so sad is, that the rest of the week she was wonderful, sold out every show, and the later reviews were great. But, the damage was done.

As bad as I felt about losing the opportunity, I felt just as bad for Helen. I knew how the business can make you bitter along the way. I refused to allow it to happen to me. I think if I hadn't gone to the war, I might have viewed things differently, but I couldn't let it get me. I never gave up on myself and I wasn't giving up on Helen. I made sure we stayed in touch. I knew I could make it work for her eventually. Helen Reddy has one of the most recognizable voices in the world, along with Karen Carpenter. The best!

Finally in 2000, I had major funding on the table for Helen after securing a deal with the Home Shopping Network for a Christmas in July project. We were also set to continue making appearances throughout the Thanksgiving/Christmas season.

I went out to L.A. and met with Helen at her home in Santa Monica. It was obvious she wasn't doing very well financially. The house was in disrepair; she rented rooms out to individual actors and actresses and was forced to sleep on a couch in her living room. It was very sad. I opened the dialogue with business first. I offered her a $25,000 non-recoupable advance and a nice piece of the net profits from record one after our recoupment of hard costs. That certainly got her attention. Then, we started discussing the creative issues.

Helen was all ears and before long began suggesting titles to record. I was thrilled. I arranged for us to meet in New York at Warner/Chappell Music. I had an administration deal with them for my catalog and both Helen and I were friends with Frank Military, a veteran music publisher going back to the days of Sinatra. Warner/Chappell had put together a multiple-CD Christmas song package for promotional use only.

Helen and I sat with Frank and selected most of the material for the project from the catalog. Helen called me the next day after listening to all the material.

"Billy," she said, "I have to record 'The Christmas of Your Life.' It's one of the best new Christmas songs I've heard in decades."

"Great," I told her. I couldn't be any happier, because I co-wrote that song with Ray Dahrouge a few years earlier.

Finally, I'm getting my Helen Reddy recording I'd wanted for over twenty years. Helen sang the song so beautifully and it's still popular every season. She worked very hard preparing for the project. We met several times and she would sing me suggestions for the arrangements. She even worked out a wonderful medley of another Terrell and Dahrouge song, "The Best Christmas Ever," with "The Most Wonderful Time of the Year."

Helen Reddy is one of the most amazing artists I've ever had the pleasure of recording. She gave me twelve finished performances in a three-hour session, which is unheard of. She had to stop and do one song over again because she started crying when she taped a photo of her granddaughter Lilly she loved so much on the microphone. When she sang the Don Costa/Bergman's song "Christmas Mem'ries," she broke down. The lyric that got to her was, *"Shiny faces of all the children, who now have children of their own."* That was all she could handle before the tears fell like rain. I came out from behind the glass to console her. We hugged, and she explained that until Lilly was born, she had been estranged from her daughter for decades. They finally found common ground. I couldn't hold back a few tears, either, as I related so well to her pain.

The Best Christmas Ever CD premiered on The Home Shopping Network in July 2000.

Helen and I enjoyed huge success on The Home Shopping Network with
our Christmas CD in 2000.

We recorded a wonderful set of Christmas songs and packaged it with a CD containing ten of her biggest pop hits that I licensed from EMI-Capitol Special Markets. Everyone said I was spinning my wheels. At that time, Helen wasn't selling much at all. I argued, "Of course not, she hasn't had a new project in decades." We went on Home Shopping and blew out ten thousand units like we were giving them away. We went back in November and did well again. Then I licensed a ten-song Christmas package to EMI-Capitol Special Markets, and they blew out over one hundred thousand units.

After our Christmas project, I almost had her convinced to revisit a standards CD. She took my hand and said, "Billy, I'm through. I'm tired of fighting with my weight, coloring my hair, and with my health issues, I just can't do it anymore." Helen had been suffering from Crones disease for some time. At that point, she moved to a small island in the South Pacific with one traffic light and became a hypnotherapist.

Ever since I first heard Frankie Avalon's smash hit "Venus" on the radio in 1959, I instinctively gravitated to music coming out of Philadelphia. Whenever I had thirty-nine cents to spare from shoveling snow or picking up bottles on the beach to take back for the deposit, I ran down to Borsetti's Market in South Belmar and bought a 45 rpm record.

Every record I bought at that time was either Frankie Avalon on Chancellor Records or it was a song written by Kal Mann and Dave Appell on Cameo-Parkway Records. Those records were nearly all by either my favorite group, The Dovells, or Bobby Rydell. As much as I idolized Avalon, Bobby inspired me more than anyone else as a performer. I loved everything he did.

In 1961 I bought my first Rydell album, *Bobby Rydell Live at the Copa*. I wore the record out on a small record player and would always sing along with "A Lot of Livin' to Do." By the summer of '62, I was all in to pursue a career in music. In the spring of '63, when I went to New York for the first time, there was a booth in the Port Authority Bus Terminal that had a recording device that allowed you to record your voice for twenty-five cents and get a small, yellow cardboard record that would play on a record player. I went in and sang "A Lot of Livin' To Do" and really liked what I heard. It was also the song I auditioned with a few months later when I signed with Vic Catala after the introduction from Clay Cole.

As with Avalon, I always felt a professional and spiritual connection to Rydell. After my success arranging and producing Avalon's disco version of "Venus," I was happy to see Bobby was offered the opportunity in '76 to record a disco version of one of his early hits on Cameo, "Sway." Frankie's success with the disco version of "Venus" was obviously the inspiration for the record deal. For decades, I hoped that one day I'd have a song of mine recorded by Bobby. And as with Avalon and Helen Reddy, my dream also was to work with him in the studio.

Then in 2003, my dream came true. Michael Marks at St. Nicholas Music hired me to produce new recordings of Johnny Marks songs with off-label, vintage artists. I reached out to Bobby immediately. I was thrilled when he agreed to the deal. I was blown away when I realized the date of our first recording session was July 16, 2003—forty years to the day of my signing my first management contract with Catala.

Bobby sang amazing versions of "A Holly Jolly Christmas," "Rockin' Around the Christmas Tree," "I Heard the Bells on Christmas Day," and a few other songs in the St. Nicholas catalog that had been underexposed. Then another milestone came my way. Bobby agreed to record "A Philadelphia Christmas," a great song Dahrouge and I wrote especially with him in mind. His performance was magnificent. From the Brill to the Brink and Back! I was 3 and 0. My greatest inspirations came full circle.

The only project I produced with Bobby we did in 2003.

Unfortunately, throughout the recording process it wasn't all fun and smiles. Bobby's head was not in a good place. He was fine until he started drinking. This was an ongoing problem he discussed at length in his recently released autobiography, *Bobby Rydell: Teen Idol On The Rocks*. I respected him too much and for too long to give him a hard time about it. Not to mention, I felt his pain. His wonderful wife,

Camille, was suffering with cancer. Tragically, she lost her battle with cancer a few years later.

I'm so happy to know Bobby's life has turned around after some challenging health issues. I remember worrying that he might never recover. The week before Camille passed away, she and the doctors convinced Bobby to go to Las Vegas to perform with his Philadelphia pals, the Golden Boys (Frankie, Bobby, and Fabian). It would do him good to get away a few days. I was sitting in the Polo Lounge at the Beverly Hills Hotel with James Darren on Friday that week, having a drink. We decided to call Avalon in Vegas to see how Bobby was doing. Frankie said Bobby completely melted down on stage the night before. Jimmy and I were willing to fly to Vegas and accompany Bobby back to Philadelphia, but Frankie said it wasn't necessary. I got back home from L.A. that Sunday night and had a doctor appointment early Monday morning. I called Bobby first thing to see how he was doing. He said Camille had passed away less than an hour before. I felt terrible because I was booked to perform on a cruise and had to leave before the funeral. I wished I could've been there for the family.

Unfortunately, Bobby continued his obsession with alcohol to the point where he nearly died. His friends rallied round him, and in 2012 he had a miracle surgery, allowing him to receive both a new liver and a new kidney in a rare double transplant. Since then, he's literally a new man and singing as great as ever.

While working on the Christmas project with Bobby, I had a few conversations with him about his career. I asked if he regretted not staying in Hollywood after appearing in the film version of *Bye Bye Birdie*. He said no, and I think he did the right thing. I reminded him of the value in raising his two wonderful children away from all that nonsense out there. I also told him I sincerely felt he was, pound for pound, the greatest all-round talent ever to come out of Philadelphia. And I meant it.

I always felt he could've easily picked up where the late, great Bobby Darin left off. I certainly believe that Bobby would've been the perfect artist to make the transition to the *Great American Songbook* in the early '90s. Unfortunately, his manager obviously didn't encourage him to move forward. I guess it was too easy to just pick up dates relying on his hits from the late '50s and early '60s.

You could argue, at the end of the day, packaging Bobby with Avalon and Fabian as The Golden Boys was no small deal. Financially it was a windfall for the guys. And they're still working the circuit and having fun. But, in my gut, Bobby Rydell should have, could have, would have easily carried the *Great American Songbook* right alongside Tony Bennett and the best in the business. All in all, to me, there will always only be "one" Bobby Rydell.

At Bobby's book signing in NYC with pals Paul Shaffer and Jerry Blavat at Patsy's Restaurant.

SIXTEEN

My Career as a Stand-up Comedian

A FEW YEARS AGO, I WAS IN L.A. HOLDING COURT AS USUAL at the Polo Lounge in the Beverly Hills Hotel. I went to use the men's room and I noticed that Adam Sandler and a friend were sitting in the lobby. I walked over, didn't even say hello. Instead I just began talking to them as if I had been sitting with them all along.

"I recently had lunch at The American Grille in Hightstown, New Jersey," I began. And I told the waitress about a Sunday evening in 1987. Sandler and his friend looked at me cockeyed. I pointed to three steps going up to a private dining area and said, "Adam Sandler and I did a comedy show on those steps and we were only making seventy dollars apiece."

Adam looked at me kind of strangely again, and I said, "I'm Billy Terrell."

He jumped out of his seat and hollered, "Billy Terrell!" and hugged me.

"You're a great man," he told me, as my eyes started to tear. "You always were there for us. You were always there for the younger guys."

I hugged him back and didn't want to let go. I was happy for his success and he was truly happy for mine.

———

I remember the very first time I ad-libbed a joke. It was 1953, when I was eight years old in Belmar, New Jersey. Back in those days, the beer companies were big advertisers on TV. Pabst Brewing Company had a commercial that went, "Pabst Blue Ribbon, the beer that made Milwaukee famous."

Well, my mother was so drunk one afternoon when we sat down to eat, she was swaying back and forth. She drank a lot of beer. I instinctively turned to my father and said, "Dad, I think Mommy is making Milwaukee famous all by herself." I thought he was going to fall off his chair.

All through my life whenever I started to get laughs, whether I was trying to be funny or not, I would take it and run with it. Sometimes to the point I couldn't turn it off. Nothing made me happier than getting laughs. Come to think of it, I lived the old adage, "Laugh and the world laughs with you, cry and you cry alone." I realize now it was my saving grace.

In early 1985, I merged my publishing catalog with Robert Williams of Spotlite Enterprises in New York City. Spotlite was a talent agency with a variety of music artists and comedians they represented. I initially met Robert when I worked on some remixes of tracks Robert's wife, Deborah, had recorded. Robert was interested in starting a music publishing company and asked me to run it. I convinced him to do a partnership deal with my contribution being 50 percent of the publishing rights of my catalog.

I never really paid much attention to what was going on with Spotlite. They had a lot of people on their roster I had never heard of at that time. I was focused on the music side of the business, but I had always been intrigued with comedy. I was very funny as a kid. Even in the midst of all the turmoil, I was a natural. I could get a laugh out of any subject. All my life, comedy was calling me.

Then one day Williams called me into his office and said he recognized my comedic talent and suggested I start working on developing an act. The comedy scene was exploding, and Spotlite dominated the landscape. I didn't realize the magnitude of the environment I found myself in. Robert arranged for me to start working out twice a week in Philadelphia: Wednesday nights at The Comedy Works on Chestnut Street and Thursday nights at The Comedy Factory Outlet on Bank Street.

My first open mike was on November 20, 1985 at The Comedy Works. It was just six days after my forty-first birthday. It was rough in the beginning. I had more than enough stage experience from performing as a musician for over twenty years at that point, but comedy was a different animal. I tried too hard to give the audience what I thought they wanted instead of just being myself. For over three months, I struggled to settle in. I never wrote anything down, though. I just went up there and made fun of my life and what was going on in the world that amused me from my perspective. I never understood sitting alone at a kitchen table trying to be funny with just the walls for an audience.

Then on March 6, 1986, prior to my spot at The Comedy Factory, I had dinner with a few music clients. I had a few drinks before dinner, wine with dinner, and Sambuca after dinner. I was very well oiled by the time I was ready to get on stage. Just before it was my turn to do my ten minutes I said to myself, "The hell with it, I'm just going to be myself; I've been funny all my life!"

At the time, I wore big plastic-rimmed eyeglasses, my dentures were fifteen years old and worn down, my hair was thinning, and I didn't look like I fit in up there at all. The minute I walked on stage, a girl in the front row pointed up to me and screamed, "The fearless fly!"

I was nice and loose from all the alcohol, and I went right after her.

"The fearless fly?" I barked back at her. "Get the fuck out of here!" I said, pointing toward the exit. The audience went wild. They roared and roared. It was like rocket fuel for me. My entire persona kicked right in. I felt like I was back in Bradley Beach, New Jersey, in 1952 when I was making crazy jokes with my mother and father howling with laughter.

At that time, The Comedy Factory had a stationary video camera for us to bring in a VHS and the sound guy would tape our sets. It was a wonderful tool for us to study what we were doing and how the audience was reacting. The following week when I walked on stage at the Factory, it was like I had been doing comedy for five years. I took command instantly. I had confidence and broke right into a more aggressive attitude, taking on the persona of everybody's crazy uncle at a family reunion.

Up to that point, I played it subdued with no profanity or edge. I guess I was trying to make the audience like me first. Kind of how I used to feel back in school, wishing people would like me. But I found my niche and it worked.

I became more confident week after week working the Philly clubs, and I started to set my sites on New York City. One Sunday night, I went up to Rodney Dangerfield's comedy club on First Avenue in Manhattan and hung around. The show that night was packed with acts working about ten to twelve minutes each. The guy running the show that evening offered me a spot and I took it. There were some very cool acts on that night that I enjoyed. I was slotted in to follow Andrew "Dice" Clay, who was known for his foul mouth. I really didn't care for it either. I walked onto the stage and adlibbed my opening line.

"Ladies and gentlemen, I would rather find something else to do before I stood in front of an audience and talked about sticking my tongue up a woman's butt in line at the bank!"

Then, I went on with my set and it went over well. They loved the character, and so did Dangerfield's partner, Tony, who ran the place. When I went to the bar after my set, Andrew "Dice" Clay was there, and it was obvious that he wasn't happy with my opening line. I really didn't care.

I learned early on if I stayed true to the character, the act worked. If I lost confidence and allowed myself to be intimidated, I was like a wounded deer destined to be done in. I certainly had my share of those experiences, but I never gave in. I had been knocked down many times in my life and it wasn't going to happen as a comedian.

I approached my comedy career like a prizefighter. I wasn't going down for anybody. You could hit me with the stool. Pound me silly. But

I wasn't going down! I was only cancelled once in all those years and I only threw the towel in once in all those years of more than twenty-four hundred performances.

In November 1986 I was only doing comedy about a year when a fellow comedian at The Comedy Factory in Philly recommended me to a club in Washington, DC. I was offered a Friday and Saturday and took the gig. Up to that point, I was still mostly just honing the act a few nights a week, ten to twelve minutes at a time.

I got to town early Friday afternoon on November 7, 1986, settled into the hotel, and had a few drinks to tune up a bit. Up to then, I hadn't visited the Wall. I made a huge mistake and walked over to the Vietnam Memorial Wall. I stood in front of the 1967 granite panel and stared at the names of the casualties. I was numb. I sat down, leaning on the wall, crying uncontrollably. What was I thinking? When I walked on for the first show on Friday, I was lost. I was empty; I did eight minutes and walked off not realizing I didn't do enough time. The manager cancelled me immediately and called another local comic in to cover the weekend.

In May of 1987, I was booked at Tracy's Comedy Club in Carney, Maryland, just outside of Baltimore. I was getting traction and working more and more clubs and establishing a nice following. I also worked downtown Baltimore at The Comedy Factory Outlet in the Inner Harbor a few times a year until around 1993 and always enjoyed it. Then, the comedy scene began to change, with many younger acts coming on the scene with filthy material and profanity just for the sake of shock value. The audiences were changing. The couples and groups of neighbors out for dinner and a few laughs weren't coming anymore. The material was too gross.

Things weren't going very well for me in 1993. By December I was faced with the reality that I needed to balance comedy with more music projects to make a living. I was booked at The Comedy Factory in Baltimore on a very cold weekend that month. I was booked for four shows (Friday and Saturday) for very nice money. The club for years was like my living room in Bradley Beach. I could do no wrong. When I walked on stage for the first show on Friday, I was confronted with a young, nasty crowd that obviously were drinking a lot before coming to the show. I wasn't completely myself to begin with, which made it worse. I just wasn't feeling it and I was getting no help from the crowd at all. For the first time, I stopped my act, sat down on a stool.

"People," I began, "I've enjoyed working here for the past six years. But tonight, I just don't have it and I can't see putting all of you and myself through this. Have a nice evening." And I walked off. But in my gut, I was humiliated. I don't go down for anybody!

The club manager was a very nice black woman who was always good to me. She wanted to pay me in full, but as much as I needed it, I refused the money. She stuck a hundred dollar bill in my pocket anyway. She clearly felt my pain.

"You're funny, Billy," she said to me, "and you've proved it over and over. It happens. Let it go!"

I walked out into the bitter cold, crying like a baby all the way to the bar down the block. I had a few drinks and walked back to my hotel. To add insult to injury, I slipped on the ice and bruised my hip so bad I couldn't stand up for a few minutes. A few people wanted to help me get on my feet, but I refused. I laid there feeling so rejected, I wasn't sure I ever wanted to get up.

All in all, my life in comedy was a dream come true. I got to travel to places I'd have never experienced otherwise. I shared the stage with amazing talent, enjoyed incredible support from loyal fans in several states up and down the East Coast, and was reminded nightly that I was accepted for who and what I was. I read a lot on the road. The younger acts were going to the mall or the movies in the afternoons and chased women at the clubs after the shows. I was in my forties and just wanted to relax.

I always enjoyed speaking with the up-and-coming acts that were intrigued by my music career and knowledge of the business in general. I remember one show in Holyoke, Massachusetts. A very young Jim

Norton was the opener. I believe it was one of his earliest gigs outside of New York City. He asked me what I thought of his act. I told him to just stay true to what he was doing. I explained his persona was right on the money so don't worry about the material. That will develop. I told him he had something special going on and he will succeed. Just stick to the game plan. I was very happy to see I was right. Several years later I opened for Jim in Reading, Pennsylvania, and we shared a thumbs up when we first saw each other that night.

I worked throughout Pennsylvania more than any other state. There were clubs everywhere in Pennsylvania. The top agents were in New York; the acts shared hotel rooms in the city and took road gigs in PA, as it was easy access in and out. I played venues that were vaudeville theaters in the '20s and '30s. Many places had the sets and costumes still there back stage. A few had the pianos from back in the day that Chico Marx and other famous performers used. I loved the history.

My act was perfect for audiences all over Pennsylvania. My material was tailor-made for all corners of the state. My Amish routine used to kill.

"What's up with these people? The Amish guy wouldn't take a picture with me. I wanted to go back to Newark and show my friends I landed on another planet. I said to guy, 'What's the matter, you don't like Italians? You dizzy-looking prick, I'll stick an ice pick in your neck.'

"Then the Amish guy would say, 'Sir, I let two guys sleep here one night, an Italian and a Puerto Rican. I got up the next day, my horse's head was gone, and my wagon was on blocks!'"

It was rough but all in fun. I took on a pseudo Joe Pesci delivery, which I was quite familiar with, having been born in Newark. What I did was so personal and relevant to my actual life experiences, I had a completely original act. Through the years, many comedians used to say to me, "Man, you're really hard to steal from."

I always told them, "I lived it. How can you possibly steal my life?"

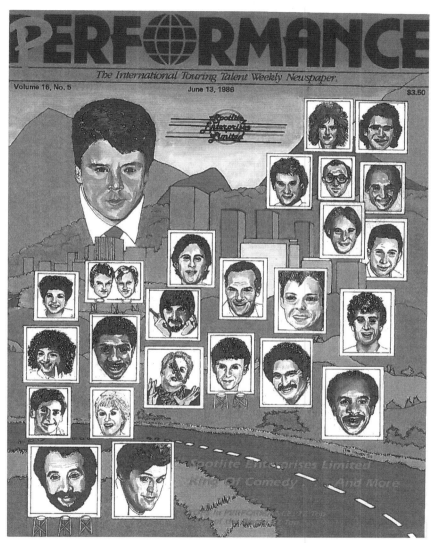

Even though I was in the earliest stages of honing my act in 1986, Robert Williams insisted on including my image on the Spotlite roster which gave me an enormous boost of credibility.

———————

Speaking of Joe Pesci, my Aunt Laura was close to Joe's sister since childhood and was even in her wedding party. Around the end of February in 1976, the Frankie Avalon record was all over the radio and was in the top ten on WOR in New York City. Aunt Laura called me one afternoon at the De-Lite Records' office saying that Joe would like to speak with me. At the time, Joe and the late Frank Vincent had a show band and were one of the hottest club acts on the Jersey circuit.

Aunt Laura said, "Cousin Joe is thinking about giving up the band and taking a chance at becoming an actor. Knowing that you're in New York and that you know Danny DeVito (who, like Joe, was also diminutive in size), he'd appreciate any advice you might have for him." Ray Dahrouge knew Danny much better than I did, but in 1971 Danny used to take the same bus from Asbury Park to New York that we did, so we talked about his quest to get into acting.

About a half hour after my aunt called, Joe called me, and we spoke for about forty-five minutes. I mentioned what I knew that Danny Devito had done. Interestingly, both Danny and Joe were barbers before getting into show business. My advice was, sign up at the American Academy of Dramatic Arts in Manhattan, subscribe to *Variety* and *Backstage* magazines, and check out the casting calls daily. I also suggested he move to the city, even if it meant he needed a roommate, but make sure to be available for last-minute opportunities. He was very appreciative.

I had heard that Joe had appeared in a film produced in Newark, but it never saw the light of day. The word was he walked away from acting and worked in Vegas in construction before being offered a job to manage a restaurant in the Bronx, possibly owned by connected guys, but I really don't know. In any event, the story goes that while they were trying to cast the role of Jake LaMotta's brother in Martin

Scorsese's film *Raging Bull,* somehow Robert De Niro got a VHS copy of the "B" movie from Newark. He called Scorsese immediately, saying he had found Jake's brother. They tracked down Joe, and De Niro called the restaurant to make a reservation for he and Marty to meet with Joe. I heard when Joe first took the call, he thought it was a joke and hung up. Then Bob and Marty showed up for dinner and the rest is history.

I lectured at Temple University for four semesters in the music department in the early '80s and told the Pesci story a few times. My point was, save all your work. Make backup copies, as every song means something, and you can never count out the possibility of your work becoming relevant when you least expect it!

———————

I worked out most of my comedy material in my car going to and from gigs. If I saw a television commercial or a news story I felt was absurd, I would rag on it in my car out loud with my stage persona taking over. Then that night or the very next time on stage, I would let it fly. Most of those routines were expanded right on stage. The more the audience laughed, the more I elaborated on the situation in character. It worked. The entire act was honest every minute. There's no way you could develop that in your kitchen.

My persona was more important than what I was saying. Very much like many icons such as Jack Benny, Don Rickles, Jackie Mason, Pat Cooper, Groucho Marx, etc. It was a lesson I learned early on, even as a child imitating the greats on the Sullivan show. My body language spoke as loud as my voice. I was destined to do comedy.

I was inspired by Jackie Gleason and *The Honeymooners* as early as 1953.
I've been blessed being friends with Joyce "Trixie" Randolph. For over twenty
years, we've met for drinks and laughs at Sardi's Restaurant and Bar on West
44th Street in the heart of the theater district in Manhattan.

The more I traveled, the more I enjoyed the process. I understand now that it was the process that was always more important to me than the money or anything else. The life was very much like vaudeville in the early twentieth century. I spoke to Jeanette Barber, who I worked with in Syracuse in the late '80s after she stopped performing to join Rosie O'Donnell as an assistant on her television show. I asked Jeanette if she missed doing comedy. She said what she missed was the life more than the comedy. I can relate to that very well.

I enjoyed working in Canada. Especially Ontario. I had great shows in Niagara Falls, Hamilton, London. They all had Yuk Yuk's Comedy Clubs in those towns. I'd go up there for a few weeks at a time. As much fun as it was, I occasionally found myself working with American guys who were living in Canada since the '60s after dodging the draft during the Vietnam War. I didn't let it show, but there were times I wanted to grab them by the throat. Most of the time I just did my show and stayed by myself during the day.

Niagara Falls was interesting. On Fridays, we used to get a lot of people from the New York side coming to the show. They were a much tougher crowd than the locals and tourists. If they weren't buying it, they let you know right away. I went over most of the time, but I had a few shows I could've lived without. One of the owners of the Yuk Yuk's chain was a big drinker. He used to host a lot of the shows, as well. He would drink black Russians to the tune of twenty-two per night. The club used to book famous acts from the U.S. on occasion. After Jimmy Walker worked the club in Niagara, he went on television and talked about Canada, saying there were no black Russians there because Donnie Coy drank them all. The late, great comedian Frank Gorshen played the club once the week after I was there. After the first show on Friday night, he was so humiliated he went back to the hotel and started packing. Donnie convinced him it would be better the rest of the weekend, so he stayed and did fine.

A few years later, I was hanging out at Sardi's with Gorshen when he was performing on Broadway in *Say Goodnight, Gracie*. I used to give him a hard time by mentioning Niagara Falls. After his third or fourth glass of straight scotch he would get louder and louder, "I don't want to talk about Niagara, Terrell. Stop it!" He was a great guy. I felt sorry for him when the show won a Tony Award and he didn't. It made no sense. It was a one-man show! Crazy.

In the late '80s, some of the hotels in the Catskill Mountains began booking midnight comedy shows billed as *The Young Comedians Showcase*. I was one of the new guys on the block so I was booked, even though I was much older than the other acts. I worked The Raleigh, Browns, The Tamarack, and even The Pines as a guest performer for Mal Z. Lawrence in his weekly Thursday night show. His audience was mostly elderly Jewish women. I wasn't sure how I would be received, but I was doing well at the other hotels, so I went for it.

I had the right material, having been married into the Jewish faith for ten years. My edge and my tag line, "Get the fuck out of here," didn't upset them in the least. I had the audience rolling with this one:

"The first Sunday morning after our wedding, my wife gave me a list of things she wanted for breakfast. When I got in my car and read the note, she wanted New York bagels, Philadelphia cream cheese, Nova Scotia lox, Jersey tomatoes, and Bermuda onions. I went back in and packed a suitcase. I went out for breakfast and came back with a tan." Then I added, *"Nine years I slept with my wife, and she only screamed once—we were being robbed!"*

That did it! Several of the elderly women started hollering my tag line with me, and the place went wild. When I walked off to a standing ovation, Mal Z. came back on stage so humiliated, he said, "In case you're interested, Billy will be here next week with the ASSHOLE SHOW." I walked over to the bar for a drink and was congratulated by the manager of the room. He said if anyone told him my show would've worked for this audience, he'd have said they were nuts. Just then, an elderly gentleman standing at the bar called me over.

"Do you know why you went over so well tonight?" he asked. "Because a comic says funny lines, a comedian says lines funny! They bought you and that's the sign of a great performer." I never forgot those words.

I enjoyed working the west coast of Florida. I got an enormous amount of material just watching the elderly people. I took every absurd thing I witnessed each day on stage and just winged it. I didn't think about it or try to organize it. I went right for it from jump.

"Folks, last night I performed a show at the senior place a few miles from here. I hung around to see how their tenants' meeting went. A woman in her late eighties stood up in the back of the room, made a fist, held it up, and hollered, 'Sex tonight for any man who can guess what I have in my hand.'

'An elephant!' an old codger cried out.

'Close enough,' she said."

And the whole place screamed with laughter.

When I started out on the comedy scene in 1985, I was forty-one years old. By 1987 I was getting enough traction to start working the road. In addition to performing a lot in Philadelphia, I did showcase at some of the key clubs in New York City, although I never felt comfortable up there. The club owners and managers were mostly failed comics that kept their hand in the business but weren't very gracious to acts starting out. I never understood that mentality.

Nevertheless, I did some spots at Catch A Rising Star, The Comic Strip, Dangerfield's, and The New York Comedy Club. The one night I enjoyed the most was at Catch A Rising Star. It was magic and pumped me up big time. Rosie O'Donnell opened, I went on second and did well, and Steve Shaffer went third, Dennis Miller went on fourth, and Sam Kinison closed the show. Sam was brilliant! He hadn't hit it big yet, but it was obvious he was on his way.

I didn't realize how blessed I was at the time to be looked up to by so many young, up-and-coming talented comedians. Many from time to time used to ask me my opinion of their material or advice on how to move forward. I was never comfortable giving too much advice. I felt, having come up the hard way in the business, that they should just be true to what they feel, listen to the audience, and stick with the game plan.

Adam Sandler:
I met Adam at the Comic Strip on 2nd Avenue in late 1987. I enjoyed what he did. He knew I was with Spotlite Entertainment, the top agency in the comedy world at that time. One night he asked me if I could get him an appointment there. The guys at Spotlite were already aware of Adam, but for one reason or another they didn't come together. They had their chance to sign him but obviously the timing wasn't right. I'm sure they recognized Adam's potential. He was great!

Ray Romano:

Also in 1987, I worked a lot with some great acts on their way up. One night in Lake Hopatcong, New Jersey, Ray Romano opened the show, I went on in the middle, and Rich Voss closed. Ray said he preferred the opening spot at that time because it gave him time to get back to New York City to do spots at several other clubs before they closed. Ray was a very focused, classy guy and hard worker. I was so happy to see him do so well. He was certainly one of the good guys.

In 1987 I worked with many up-and-coming comedians, including
Ray Romano and Rich Voss.

Chris Rock:

In 1988, Chris wasn't quite up to speed yet. I remember one night at Catch A Rising Star, he became very frustrated with the audience and actually said, "Come on people, what do you want?" A few months later, I was booked at Jimmy's Comedy Alley in Bayside, New York. I opened the show, Chris went second, and Gary DeLena closed. I sat with Chris in the green room a bit and we discussed our material. We both agreed that we could never buy jokes from other comics, which was quite common those days. Rodney Dangerfield and Joan Rivers used to buy material all the time for twenty-five dollars a joke. Chris, like myself, could only deliver his own material. It had to come from inside of him, or it didn't mean anything. He was a real nice kid and enjoyable to talk to.

Drew Carey:
Drew was one of the most dedicated acts on the road in the late '80s and early '90s. He had all his belongings in his car; he had a post office box in Cleveland that his sister would clean out once a week and FedEx all his mail to whatever hotel he was staying in. He traveled with a VCR and tons of his favorite movies on video. The first thing he would do when he checked into a hotel was to hook his VCR up to the television. He booked himself fifty-two weeks a year and went for it.

I only worked with Drew once, but we worked in a few towns at the same time in different clubs. In 1988 at a club outside of Philadelphia, I opened the show, Drew went on second, and the late, great Richard Jeni closed. It was a magical weekend. We did two shows on Friday and two on Saturday. Drew was making one hundred dollars a show. After the second show on Saturday night, Richard said, "Hey guys, let's go back up and sing doo-wop for a while." I could kick myself for not videotaping my shows that weekend. Rich, Drew, and I held the crowd there for another forty-five minutes, singing doo-wop songs and taking turns on lead vocals. It was incredible. The club owner gave us each twenty-five dollars extra for keeping the crowd there drinking.

After the show, Richard and I went to a diner and sat and talked until 5:00 a.m. about life, the business of comedy, and where we thought it would all lead. Very interesting guy. I was scheduled to open for Richard in March of 2007 at a corporate date in Long Island, New York. I was stunned on Sunday morning the week before the gig to get a call telling me Richard had committed suicide. He shot himself in the bathtub. Unbelievable!

Pat Cooper:

I enjoyed Pat Cooper back in the early '60s, seeing him on various television shows. My father loved Pat too. Very funny guy. I was thrilled when I was booked on a show with him in Mountainside, New Jersey, at a place called "L'Affaire." I forget who opened that night, but I went on second and had a great show. It was my audience all the way, as it was Pat's. When I came off stage and went back in the green room, Pat went out of his way before he went on to shake my hand and say, "You're marvelous!" Hearing him say that was one of the great moments along the way.

I was blessed to have had the opportunity to share the stage with Joe Piscopo and Pat Cooper back in the day.

Jackie Mason:

I never worked with Jackie as a comedian, but I did open for him with my music show at Dangerfield's on December 26 and 27 in 1982. As with Pat Cooper, I admired Jackie ever since seeing him on *The Ed Sullivan*

Show back in the late '50s. He wasn't doing very well at that time. He was working for eleven dollars a head at the door. No guarantee. His manager at the time even asked me if I could be of assistance getting them a literary agent for a book he had written.

My show went over okay, not great. It got better the second night, and I was pleased that Jackie acknowledged that I was much more comfortable than the opening night. He said, "Finishing strong is most important anyway, so don't worry about it."

Interestingly, a few years later, Jackie landed a deal to do his show on Broadway that was extremely successful. I remember someone asking him what made the difference between working for a piece of the door a few years earlier and making so much money now. His reply was, "Listen, if you take a nothing painting off your kitchen wall and place it in a museum, suddenly, it's art." I still see Jackie on occasion at Patsy's Restaurant or the Apple Diner on Broadway and always enjoy it. I always begin doing an impression of him on the Sullivan show.

Along the way, I worked with many acts that landed spots on television and movies. George Wallace, Brian Regan, Jim Norton, Angel Salazar, Andrew "Dice" Clay, Joe Piscopo, and many others. Below are some of my key routines from my twenty-four hundred shows.

"My name is Billy Terrell, ladies and gentlemen. I'm from Newark, New Jersey. I'm the only guy that got to Vietnam and felt it was an improvement!"

"My father had a rather strange outlook on life. He hardly worked a day in his life but always had a smile on his face. His philosophy was, if I can't make ten million, then the hell with it. I ain't gonna do nothing."

"He drove my mother crazy. We were evicted fifty-eight times. I used to have to call home after school for directions. One time, we got evicted on garbage day, and we lost all our furniture. I came home from school one day and asked my mother if my friend Harold could sleep over. She said, 'Billy, we're not even sleeping over!'"

"In 1953 we had a black and white Philco television that broke down all the time. It had tubes that used to get so hot you could cook breakfast on top of the television and watch Captain Kangaroo *at the same time. One Sunday evening a tube blew out, and from the middle of the screen to the top was black. My father threw a fit. I said to him, 'It's Sunday night and Lassie's always at the bottom of the screen anyway.' We didn't watch* Bonanza; *we watched Cartwright's crotch! I didn't know the Lone Ranger wore a mask until I was twenty-eight."*

"Now that I'm in my seventies, I feel myself slowing down quite a bit. I spoke to my doctor and he suggested Cialis. I said, 'I'll see anybody at this point!'"

"I do a lot of material about how simple television was in the '50s and '60s. How we had three main channels and more than enough to watch. Today we have cable with five hundred channels and nothing to watch."

"The Weather Channel kills me. The music will put you in a coma. The guy comes on and tells me it's sprinkling in Spokane. I'm an alcoholic in South Jersey. Tell me it's raining scotch, I'll get me a tin cup and a bus ticket."

"One Monday morning, I had to be in Secaucus around ten o'clock, so I decided to turn on The Weather Channel, as it's an hour-and-a-half drive. This bum comes on and tells me that it's 68 degrees in Brussels today. I don't even know where Brussels is. I'm going to help my cousin dump a body in the weeds."

After I had my first heart procedure in 2005, I thought about taking my cholesterol routine out of the show. I decided to keep it in.

"I don't know how you folks feel, but I think cholesterol is a communist plot. We didn't have cholesterol in the '50s. We put butter in coffee. We ate cows before they were dead. Now when I go to my doctor, I put on a suit and tie and walk in with The Wall Street Journal. *I say, 'Take the blood. I could care less.' Thirty minutes later, he runs out and says, 'My God, your cholesterol is 259!' I said, 'SHOULD I SELL?'*

The Food Network also gets huge laughs.

"Did you ever watch the Food Network? How bored do you have to be to sit there and watch somebody make an omelet? That's a real exciting show. Hey Gladys, take the porno back, we have a Greek salad coming up in a few minutes!"

———————

I always considered my life in comedy as "living the dream." The reward for me was the satisfaction of recognizing my calling and following through. For me, comedy was a million dollar education of hands-on experience in psychology, history, geography, and human nature that I was never afforded in my teens.

Unlike many of the comedians I worked with all those years, I was never burdened with a sense of urgency. I was comfortable in my own skin. I was always the type of performer who felt that "the drink and the laughs are on me." Many of those younger comedians felt like they had to appear on *The Tonight Show* or play Vegas by the time they turned thirty or they would never be successful. For me, more than twenty-four hundred performances and all the friends I made along the way is my definition of success.

SEVENTEEN

The Women in My Life

I DIDN'T HAVE VERY MANY GIRLFRIENDS ALONG THE WAY and after the war was no exception. A few weeks after coming home from Vietnam, I went down to Steve Brody's nightclub on the strip in Asbury Park to say hello and hear The Jaywalkers, a band I had known since 1959 in Belmar. I was sitting at the bar listening to the guys and I noticed a beautiful blond girl across the room staring at me. I stared back for a bit and then looked away, not thinking much of it. A few minutes later, she walked up and said, "I love you." I was stunned. I didn't know what to make of it. I was incredibly attracted to her, though. We talked for a bit and when she said she was the guitar player's wife, I figured well, that's that.

She was on my mind constantly after that chance meeting. She was every girl I had ever wanted wrapped up in one beautiful, petite package. She had a beautiful face, long blond hair, and eyes to die for. The following week I went down to the club again and started hanging out there regularly. The Jaywalkers were booked for several weekends. I saw Mari Anne again and mentioned that I had rented a small office in town where I was writing songs. A few days later, she stopped by my office one afternoon. She said she would be happy to help me with whatever I needed. She started coming to visit several days a week. We ultimately started kissing but nothing else, and I never touched her inappropriately. I was convinced I was in love with her, but with her being married, it was obvious that we weren't going anywhere. I never forgot her, though. At one point, our relationship became a big problem when some people told her husband I was fooling around with her. No one, not even her husband, believed that we weren't having sex. So that was it. At that point, it was best to just walk away for all concerned.

A few months later, I believe late August or early September, the realities of the difficulties of trying to adjust back to normal life after the war set in. That's when I fell deeply into alcohol. Many friends at Steve Brody's would keep buying me drinks all night, every night. I guess they felt sorry for me, as my pain was easy to recognize. At one point, I was up to twenty-two drinks a night. How I survived I'll never know. I hit bottom. I lost a girl I really loved, I was having trouble relating to the social climate in the country, and I felt like a fish out of water. Everything was catching up with me. Nineteen sixty-seven might have been the "Summer of Love" but certainly not for me.

The following five years I rarely got involved with girls. I didn't have a driver's license or a car. My clothes weren't very nice, and I looked like death warmed over. It was Manasquan High revisited. I was technically a homeless veteran by today's standards. The difference was that I didn't do drugs and had parents that cared. I slept and showered at my parents' house when I wasn't sleeping at the office. There were times if I didn't come home for a night or so, my father and brother Richie would drive around looking for me. Often, they would find me sitting in the bushes by the lake on 5th Avenue in Asbury, sipping on Cold Duck, rat gut wine, right out of the bottle, staring out as if I were back on perimeter guard in Tuy Hoa. I was a mess.

Many evenings I would hang out at Jack's Bar on Cookman Avenue, pounding down Seagram's Seven and soda. I became very friendly with the girl working behind the bar. She was a pretty blond whose nickname was Chickie. She obviously felt sorry for me and often would slip me extra drinks. She admitted later that she watered down some of the drinks, for my sake. Some nights she would even go out of her way to drive me to my parents' house, knowing I'd never make it otherwise.

I had known Chickie's family since 1961, when we first moved back to Bradley Beach. Her sister Barbara was a tomboy and used to play great basketball with us all the time. I knew about Chickie and always thought she was beautiful but out of my league. Interestingly, she was Dahrouge's childhood sweetheart and was dating Larry Oxley (Jersey Beatles) in '67 around the time I got home from Vietnam. All the time I hung out at the bar, I never thought of her romantically. She was just one of the bar crowd.

In December of '71, after Dahrouge and I went our separate ways, I was offered the opportunity to join a band called The Spice of Life. They needed an organ player, and I needed to start making a living. The job was to start the first week in February. For the next two months, I worked day and night to teach myself how to play the organ well enough to get the job, and I did. It felt good. I was making a steady living, finally got a driver's license, and bought an old '62 Cadillac. I still resembled Charles Manson, but it worked for the job.

Even though I was working four to six nights a week, I still got up a few mornings very early and went to New York to pitch my songs. I would take the 9:00 a.m. bus from Asbury and the 6:00 p.m. bus back in time to freshen up and be on the bandstand on time. One morning I got on the bus and sat down next to a girl with short brown hair holding camera equipment. She was on her way to class at the New York Institute of Photography. Interestingly, that's where I posed for students for free in 1963 to get my 8 x 10 glossy. We started talking, and a few minutes later I realized it was Chickie. She didn't recognize me at first either. We had a nice chat, talked about me now being in a band, and said goodbye. Later that day, we wound up on the same bus back and again sat next to each other, chatting. When we got to Asbury, I asked she if she needed a ride home. She said she would appreciate it and then asked if she could tag along to hear the band. I was fine with it, so she did.

Initially, we were just buddies. She enjoyed coming to some gigs a few nights a week and I enjoyed hanging out with her. Afterwards, I would take her home, and most nights she invited me to come in for tea and chat. It was all very innocent. I still felt like I was out of her league and never thought of her romantically. After about a month or so, one night we were having tea and talking as usual when she excused herself for a few minutes. Then she called out to me from her bedroom and asked if I wanted to see something. I walked in and there she was lying naked on the bed. I was quite taken back at first. I immediately imagined how Ralph Kramden in *The Honeymooners* would have reacted and under my breath I said, "OH BABY," and proceeded with the festivities. I was twenty-seven years old and it was my first experience with big-time sex. There was plenty available, and I took advantage of it. I'd never been more comfortable and confident, so I went with it. The fact that she reminded me of Tuesday Weld didn't hurt either. WOW!

With all due respect, as with many new relationships, the following few months were very exciting. I became more and more comfortable and started to feel a sense of commitment as the weeks went by. I was starting to sleep over several nights a week and before long, I became very fond of her daughter, Carrie, who up to that point hadn't known her biological father. She was so cute and a real nice kid. It wasn't long before we were living like a family together. We began discussing getting a nicer house and possibly getting married at some point.

I rented a nice house in Allenhurst one street over from Deal, which was a very affluent community. I was working steadily with the band, making a good living and began getting traction in New York again as a writer/ producer. At first everything seemed to be normal. Nice house, sweet stepdaughter, and a loving relationship. But after a few months, it became more and more apparent that it was a mistake. This life wasn't for Chickie. She was not domesticated. She had been a free spirit since she was fifteen. It was so obvious she wasn't happy with the idea that this was it. I felt horrible and used to take long walks and cry. Rejection again! Damn it!

By the fall of '73, we had been living together for a year and a half, and Carrie was repeatedly asking when we were getting married. She even called me Daddy, which I loved. I couldn't do enough to make her happy. Several times she would sit on my lap with her arms around me and say, "You're going to marry Mommy, aren't you?"

Heartbreaking! Both Chickie and I knew it was over at that point but couldn't bring ourselves to tell Carrie. So, on December 3, 1973, we were married. Being married only made things worse. Before long, Chickie was completely out of control.

We had fight after fight, to a point it was an extremely unhealthy environment for Carrie. Her mother would call the police for no reason and scream at them to take me away. Allenhurst was a very conservative town, and the police didn't like the way I looked with the long hair and beard, to begin with. Finally, in September '74, one night I had gotten home late from the studio in New York, poured a drink, put on headphones, and began listening to a reel-to-reel tape of the music I'd recorded that day. Suddenly, I hear this pounding on the front door. It's two thirty in the morning; I couldn't imagine who it was. I open the door and it was the police informing me that they had gotten a disturbance call. A moment later, Chickie came out of the bedroom and started screaming at them to take me away, I was a bum. I was shocked.

No matter how I tried to convince the police I hadn't done anything to provoke the situation, they didn't want to hear it. They dragged me out by the hair, threw me in the backseat of their car, and drove me to Asbury Park, where they dumped me on the sidewalk in front of a fleabag hotel. They told me to check in, sleep in the street if necessary, but don't come back to Allenhurst. I lost everything. My name was on the lease, and I couldn't afford to pay for two places. Eventually they were evicted and that was it. We weren't officially divorced, though, until four years later. Losing my relationship with Carrie was the worst part of it all. I still consider her my stepdaughter and always will.

After having to abandon my home and stepdaughter, I felt like the biggest loser of all time. Fortunately, the band stuck by me. They were amazing. All I had were the clothes on my back. The police threatened me so bad I couldn't go back to recover anything. My clothes, my piano, tape recorder, not even my toothbrush. We were sharing Chickie's car, so I didn't have transportation either. I realize now that I was suffering from severe PTSD. The only thing holding me together enough to function was the band. We played several nights a week. I don't know if I'd have survived otherwise.

I found myself living like a homeless vet again. At least I was working and supporting myself but everything else smelled of PTSD. I rented a rundown cottage on a dirt road in Mantoloking, New Jersey, that was convenient for the band to pick me up and drive me home after the gigs. The place was very old with a grate in the doorway between the kitchen and front room with a furnace below. When the heat was on the grate got red hot. I had to jump over it or fry myself to pieces.

I slept in an army jacket with a bush hat pulled over my face and a knife next to my pillow. I nailed all the windows shut. I even nailed the front door shut every night before going to bed. I used to do a routine in my show about those days and said, *"I missed a doctor appointment one morning because I couldn't find my claw hammer."*

All I had in the fridge was beer and a quart of milk, most of the time. My nightmares were so bad I would wake up ghost white and stumble to the 7-Eleven a few blocks away for coffee and settle myself down. The owner was a cigar-smoking character that looked more like he belonged at the racetrack than working at 7-Eleven. One morning I looked so bad, when I put my dollar on the counter to pay for the coffee, he stared at me for about twenty seconds and then pushed the dollar back to me. He said, "Forget it, pal. You'll never see lunch. The last one's on me."

I got a lot of good material for my stand-up routine from those days, though.

"I wiped my feet before I walked out."
"The rats tried to have me evicted."
"Flies repaired the holes in the window screens."
"I used to sit on a broken beach chair and read in the front yard with a beer. One day, I went inside to use the bathroom, forgetting it was garbage day. I came out and the chair was gone, and I chased the truck down the block to get it back."

Living proof that a lot of comedy is related to tragedy. Nevertheless, after a few months, I returned to the mirror for guidance and reminded myself of the fifty-eight-thousand-plus men and women whose lives were taken in 'Nam. Once again, it was like instant rocket fuel.

I started by having the band members help me bring my organ home, so I could start writing again on our off days. I focused on R&B, my strong suit. I was inspired, and it felt great. I was taking the bus to New York at least twice a week, making the rounds and making progress. By the spring of '75, I was on the charts again! "I've Always Had You" by Benny

Troy did well enough to lead to an album deal with De-Lite Records. I was back and never looked back!

Marriage #2:

As life continued to improve, the busier I became and the less I dwelled on my first marriage falling apart. I stayed pretty much to myself and didn't go out with any women at all for many months. I wasn't a one-night guy and was never interested in the groupie mentality. Then on November 15, 1975, my entire life took an amazing turn. That was the day Frankie Avalon recorded my disco version of "Venus" for De-Lite Records. Prior to going to the studio that day, Frankie and I were having breakfast in the coffee shop at the Marriot Hotel on City Line in Philadelphia. I couldn't help noticing a very pretty blond girl across the room sitting with a friend and a little girl.

They were staring at our table as it was obvious that they recognized Frankie. I went over to their table and introduced myself. The little girl was her daughter, who was five years old. She was so great. I explained that we were recording a new version of Frankie's hit song "Venus" and that they were welcome to join us at the session. They took me up on the offer and spent the afternoon enjoying the recording session. That was the beginning of a nice friendship.

Lana was divorced and seeing a real nice guy who owned an auto parts business with his brother. I was recording a lot in Philly after De-Lite Records built their own studio there. I practically lived at the Marriot so when I was in town, I called Lana and we would have dinner or lunch. As with my first marriage, everything was simply innocent and friendly. We enjoyed each other's company. After about six months, we grew much closer. I was crazy about her all along, but she was seeing someone, so I didn't feel compelled to interfere with her relationship. However, Lana became more and more comfortable with me, so we started officially dating and sharing incredible kisses.

By the fall of '76, she was ready to move out of her parents' house with her daughter, Jessica, to a town house in Norristown, Pennsylvania, just outside of Philly. Up to that point, I would come down to see her often, whether I was recording or not. The relationship wasn't without some problems, but we hung in there. I wasn't making a lot of money, even though it looked like it with Frankie's record all over the place. Plus there was a culture gap that was evident, she being Jewish and educated and me—well, what can I say? We are all products of our environment. I was disappointed, though, because I am not a dumb guy. There were times it was clear her family wasn't comfortable with me. I understood how they felt and just tried harder to win their confidence.

So, when it came time for Lana and Jess to move, I pitched in. It took a few days, so I stayed over at the town house. I was living in Belmar at the time, which was quite a haul to Norristown. She wanted me to stay and I wanted to stay, so I did. We were living together. Once again, I was so happy bonding with Jessica. At first, she was a bit withdrawn and not sure where all this would lead. But before long, we were pals. We bought her a puppy and I used to play games with her all the time. Monopoly was the most fun. We laughed like crazy. After living as a family for a few months, the subject of marriage was discussed.

As with Chickie, I realize now that Lana and I also knew it was a mistake. But on July 2, 1977, we were married in her sister's yard with many friends and family on hand. My friends that came were all Honeymooners fans. I kept the lines coming the entire day. It wasn't a good way to begin a marriage. Lana was livid. Her grandmother, who I really liked, resembled Ralph Kramden's mother-in-law to a "T." She even hated Lana's father and didn't make any bones about it. Her name was Rachel, which was perfect. My friends were on the floor when she showed up and I said, "Rachel . . . you've come back." The moment we were pronounced man and wife, I turned to my friend Ebbie and said,

"Get the bag!" It's a miracle the marriage didn't vaporize that day, right on the spot.

I was working a lot in New York, so living in Norristown wasn't working. Two and a half hours each way was a grind. I didn't want to take Jessica too far away from her father, who lived in Philadelphia and wasn't seeing her very much as it was. So we rented a house in Cherry Hill, New Jersey, just across the river from Philly. Then a year later, we bought a home in the same neighborhood to keep Jess in the same school and near her friends. I loved Jess so much. We had a lot of laughs. I used to go out with her and her friends on Halloween and act like a total maniac. One year I put one of her ballerina dresses upside down on my head and took my guitar with us. The rock group KISS was very popular at that time, so I went out as Hug. It was ridiculous. Some people looked out the window and wouldn't open the door. I was notorious in the community. Anything for a laugh.

As time went on, Lana and I had more and more problems. I felt bad about it, but it didn't seem like anything would make her happy. I was starting to struggle financially by 1980. I had a huge disco hit with my song "Rio De Janeiro" in '78 and had a good run in the genre, but I wasn't being paid. My music sold much better in Europe, and I wasn't seeing the money. We hung in there, but before long we were in rough financial shape. We did ultimately take out a second mortgage and brought everything current with a few bucks left over. But the damage was done. If it weren't for Jessica, the marriage would have folded at that time. Frankly, it probably should've, for everyone's sake.

Sadly, in July of '86, Lana said she wanted out. I knew it wasn't all her fault; the music business had changed drastically in the early '80s, and I was determined to stay with it. I'd have given in to any other demands. But my life's work was not on the table. I refused to leave the house, though. I moved into the third bedroom and continued to pay the bills.

I wasn't going anywhere, and I didn't want another divorce. For nine months, we lived together, apart. As with Carrie, I didn't want to lose Jessica. I wanted to be able to see her graduate high school and go to college. I was heartbroken when I realized that would never happen.

By January of '87, the atmosphere at home was becoming very unhealthy for Jess, so I gave in and agreed to sell the house and move on. I moved out March 15, and we closed the sale on April 1, 1987. I started drinking excessively again and was dominated by bitterness and violent nightmares, just like back in Mantoloking after my first divorce.

The difference was, this time I didn't need the mirror. I had a growing career in comedy.

Instead of feeling sorry for myself, I put a limit back on my alcohol consumption and hit the road. Comedy was booming by then, and I took full advantage of it.

The divorce was final in September. I didn't contest it because it made no sense. Once again, my work was the best medicine to ease the pain of divorce. I even made jokes about my marriages, as my act was all about my life anyway. I didn't have to write jokes. I lived them, and audiences ate it up.

Marriage #3:

After being alone for over two years after the divorce from Lana, I briefly dated a beautiful girl, but it didn't work out. She had been a top model in Italy and France in the '70s and was a Hollywood actress for a while. We were introduced by her sister, who was a songwriter who pitched me her music from time to time. At first, I really enjoyed seeing her. It was the spring of '89. I was very busy and doing well. It felt good to have a relationship again.

Unfortunately, in less than two months, it was obvious she had a lot of problems. I realized she was smoking pot and taking huge pills that would put her in a trance. I've always hated drug abuse and there was no way I would tolerate it. I felt sorry for her, and myself, but I had to cut her loose.

Shortly after I stopped seeing her, I was driving back from a gig in western Pennsylvania through East Stroudsburg. I was asking myself, *When am I going to find the right woman to share my life with? Will it ever happen?* Then, I remembered meeting Mrs. Ann two years earlier at one of my shows. She was a fortune teller and palm reader who was amazing. I remember her telling me she lived near East Stroudsburg. She was an incredible psychic. I decided to look her up while I was in the area. I found her place and went in to talk to her. Once again, she nailed it! She told me about a recent failed relationship and how I'm much better off that it happened. Then Mrs. Ann told me to relax because there is someone in my near future who will be so perfect for me and supportive for the rest of my life. She went on to describe the woman as someone who was completely opposite of anyone I'd ever been attracted to before.

Ever since I was a teenager, I loved blond actresses. I adored Tuesday Weld, Sandra Dee, and Carol Baker. Amazingly about a year later, September 1990, a friend of mine who owned a financial services firm called to say he just hired a girl he thought I would like. I wasn't sure I was ready, but I did ask her to dinner a month later. We went to Olive Garden on Halloween night. I used to do a joke after that, saying, *"She never took her mask off, but she seemed awfully nice!"*

She reminded me of Teresa Wright, a great actress who appeared in one of my favorite films of all time, *The Best Years of Our Lives*. At first, I wasn't sure I wanted to get involved, but at dinner that night we talked for hours until the place closed. My health wasn't good at all from all the road work and drinking. I ran myself in the ground. I was constantly in the emergency room thinking this was it. But, Elizabeth and I just clicked. She was incredibly supportive and understanding.

From that night until this day we've been together. Elizabeth saved my life. I've never experienced the level of loyalty and support I continue to get from Elizabeth.

In 2005, I began having serious health issues due to Agent Orange exposure in the war. Once again, I was reminded, the war never ended for me. Elizabeth was the saving grace through it all. Two cancers, two heart procedures, two TIAs (Transient Ischemic Attacks), and horrible PTSD. God Bless Her!

All my life, I've heard expressions like "six degrees of separation" and "some things are just meant to be." I guest there is some truth to it. When I first visited Elizabeth's parents in Kearny, New Jersey, her mother brought out photo albums of her family. As I was glancing through the album, I said, "Wait a minute. I have this photo." It was a photo of Elizabeth with the Easter Bunny at Steinbach's department store in Newark in 1952. My Aunt Laura took me to the same store that year at Easter time and had my picture taken with the same bunny. On the back of Elizabeth's photo, her mother wrote "Betty, Easter 1952." Aunt Laura wrote "Billy, Easter 1952" on mine. We were probably in line the same day. Everything was identical: the bunny's pose, the lighting and back drop. Unbelievable!

We were married on December 19, 1992.

EIGHTEEN

Returning to the Orphanage in 2013

I TOOK MANY PHOTOS AT THE ORPHANAGE IN 1966. I HAD them developed in a small store in the village of Tuy Hoa and kept them in plastic. A few I sent home, but I really didn't write very much, and I only received two letters the entire time in Vietnam. One came from my mother shortly after Thanksgiving. She wrote that the turkey didn't taste the same without me at the table. The guys ribbed me for days. They'd call out, "There goes Torsiello the turkey man." I got one short letter from my father, but I don't remember much about it. I think I was in the hospital and out of it.

I kept the photos in a plastic bag and never looked at them for over forty years. I just didn't want to think about Vietnam at all, even though I loved those babies so much and would've taken all of them home if it were possible. Leaving them there broke my heart. I think that's why I couldn't look at those faces. The memories and nightmares of the war itself were horrible, but thoughts of those babies were unbearable.

I had decades of nightmares, mostly related to the screams of the casualties arriving at the 8th Field Hospital every night or from holding babies with severe napalm burns. Instinctively, I'd hit the ground if a car backfired or I heard any loud, unexpected sound. It would shock me right back to the war mentally. I couldn't imagine ever returning to Vietnam. I never gave it a second thought.

For over forty years, 1967–2008, I moved so many times to various environments for a variety of life changing circumstances, whether it was for financial difficulties, divorces, alcohol, and/or PTSD symptoms clouding my better judgment. Along the way, I lost many items I wish I had back today, especially my uniform and ribbons I wore home from the war. A huge regret to this day.

I remember the day they announced that all search and destroy combat missions were being suspended as the Paris peace talks were beginning to bear fruit. It was obvious the war was winding down with America on the short end of the stick. I was so distraught, I wrapped up everything I brought back from the war in a large garbage bag and put it out on the curb. I kept saying to myself, "All that, for what? To cut and run? BULLSHIT!"

Fortunately, at that time my photos from 'Nam were still at my parents' house and were safe. I took them with me when I moved into my home in Cherry Hill in 1977 with my second wife and stepdaughter. But I still wouldn't open that plastic bag for another thirty-one years. Then one day in 2008, I was at my desk and out of the blue decided to Google Mang Lang Orphanage just to see what would happen. I never expected to find anything but there it was! Amazing! There were several links to articles about organizations like Airline Ambassadors supporting orphanages all over South Vietnam, including Mang Lang. I was elated!

When I got home that night I went in the closet and got out the canvas bag I kept all my photos and the birthday cards my mother and I had exchanged for many years until her death in 1989. I finally opened the plastic bag with all the photos from 1966 at Mang Lang Orphanage. I had totally forgotten how amazing they were. I stared at them for hours reminiscing and wondering how they made out after fall of South Vietnam.

A few days later, I decided to reach out to Airline Ambassadors. I spoke with one of the women who had participated in several excursions back to Vietnam, bringing school supplies and funds to help feed the orphans. John Scheer and I met her in Washington, DC, a few months later. I had several of my photos touched up and made copies to bring to her to take back to Mang Lang in 2009. She did, and I was able to find a nice article online about their visit to Mang Lang with photos of the staff and a few of my babies still there, now in their fifties, in wheelchairs. When I read that it was the first time they ever saw pictures of themselves as children, I lost it.

When I heard that the North Vietnamese destroyed all photos and written material when they raided our orphanage in Tuy Hoa in 1975 after the fall of Saigon, I cried. I was also heartbroken to learn that all the boys over the age of twelve were taken away and forced into slave labor in the rice fields and never heard from again. I found myself once again back in the war. Waking up in the night in a cold sweat, thinking of my little buddy, Tung, who screamed bloody murder every time I had to leave the orphanage and get back to base camp. How was he? Did he survive? Was he tortured? I was experiencing one of the most bittersweet moments of my life. I had to know more. I knew then I had to return to Vietnam eventually.

I got together with my dear friend and associate filmmaker Laurence Caso to discuss the possibility of doing a documentary about my experiences. I was ready to come out of the shadows, and it felt good. We immediately followed up with the people at Airline Ambassadors. They put us in touch with Sister Modestine, one of the nuns at Mang Lang in '66. She was living near Oakland, California, and going back and forth to Vietnam to help the nuns and orphans at several locations.

After more than four years of research and working on the concept of *The Other Side of War,* we were fortunate enough to be introduced to Thanh Armagost, a Vietnamese woman married to an American since the early '70s, living in western Pennsylvania. Thanh is an extraordinary woman who had been returning to Vietnam six times a year with Doctors Without Borders, an organization that funds excursions with physicians who volunteer their time and services to help sick children all over South Vietnam. Wonderful people. Thanh loved my story and agreed to help us.

Thanh went to see Sister Michelle, who was in a nursing home in Quy Nhon. She showed her some of my photos and it was game on! Then we began planning to go to Vietnam in November of 2013, which we did. Thanh worked everything out for us. She arranged for our visas, travel plans, lodging, and a van driver, and even stayed an extra week after her Doctors Without Borders excursion to be with us the entire time. We arrived in Ho Chi Minh City on the 13th of November 2013 and went to Tuy Hoa the next day to visit the principal and staff at the building we established in 1966. It was unbelievable.

My dear friend and producer/director Laurence Caso and I visited the now daycare center in Tuy Hoa on November 13, 2013. We gave the director a $500 cash donation for the children.

Our original building had gone through renovations and expansion a few times over the years. It was great seeing our 1966 plaque still survived.

The building is now a government-run daycare center. Over the years, it's been expanded so much I hardly recognized it except for our original 1966 plaque still over the front door. Thanh had informed the staff of our visit, so they prepared refreshments and decorated the dining hall with balloons and flowers. We took photos with the staff, including one with me making a $500 cash donation to the principal. Then I was taken to each of the five classrooms to meet all the wonderful children, all dressed in their school uniforms.

As I visited each classroom, the children all formed a circle and sang "Happy Birthday" to me in English. I had just turned sixty-nine. It was an incredibly emotional day. They also made me paper flowers with each classroom number on them. It was impossible to hold back the tears. I flashed back to '66 several times that afternoon. Those angels were so beautiful. I was wiping the tears away.

That night we stayed at the CenDeluxe Resort Hotel on the south end of Tuy Hoa near the causeway bridge overlooking rice paddies. It was as chilling as driving across the bridge during the war when it was oh, so dangerous. But there I was in a five-star hotel and a beautiful hotel room, looking at all the familiar locations. It was very comfortable until about 2:00 a.m., when a heavy thunder and lightning storm came through. I freaked out.

The lightning lit up the rice paddies like back in the day when I was on perimeter guard. It put me back in the war, ghost white and shaking. I closed the curtains and went down to the lobby to email my PTSD counselor at the veterans center in Trenton, New Jersey. She helped me with breathing exercises and talked me down slowly. Thank God!

The next day we went to Tuy An to see the original Mang Lang location and meet the staff and the orphans. Sister Michelle, who was living in a nursing home in Quy Nhon, came down, and we shared the greatest reunion you could ever imagine and got it all on video. Four of my babies from '66 were there, and they were amazing. Sadly, three were in wheelchairs and one was in the mental ward. Their love and affection was so heartwarming. I felt an amazing sense of closure I longed for all those years!

With Sister Michelle and Ahn Doe, who was only eight years old in 1966 when we helped establish the new orphanage.

It was an incredible reunion with four of my babies still living at Mang Lang Orphanage after all these years. Especially on my sixty-ninth birthday in 2013 in Tuy An, Vietnam.

189

Four of these girls in this 1966 photo are in my 2013 reunion photo in Tuy An.

For many years after the war, I avoided any Vietnam war movies. I just didn't want to go there. I buried myself in my work in the late '60s, and I was locked into a do-or-die attitude. Never give up, no matter what. I remember my friend Ebbie, who I also used to write with, asking me about it one night.

"Billy, you're a smart guy," he began. "What if you put yourself through all this and you don't make it?"

"Well, I'll never know because I'll die trying."

More importantly, I had deep respect for the opportunity to go on, knowing that no matter what I accomplished, nothing would be as important to me as sparing my mother a broken heart. It wasn't until shortly after my second divorce, when I was so distraught about having to walk away from my home, a wonderful stepdaughter, and a peaceful suburban lifestyle that I never had as a child, that I gave in and went to see *Platoon* with Charlie Sheen. Huge mistake.

My head was so messed up. I guess in a way I wanted to torture myself for not seeing that the divorce was inevitable. At first, I was numb watching so many familiar scenes. Especially being able to relate to individual personalities of most of the members of the platoon. I instinctively knew Gardner wasn't going to make it the moment he came on the screen. I cried when he took his last breath. On the other side of all of that, I did walk out of the theater with some important lessons.

Two scenes made a lasting impression on me to this day. One was just before the huge fight started toward the end of the film when the black soldier got his orders to leave 'Nam at the last minute. The tearful camaraderie between him and Charlie Sheen's character was most moving. He said to Sheen, "Listen, man, all you have to do is make it out of here, and it's all gravy." All gravy! God, did I relate to that.

The other scene was at the end when Sheen's character was on the chopper leaving the battlefield saying he felt that it was his responsibility to go on and make something of himself, out of respect for the people he left behind. That scene, that moment, brought me right back to my mother's bathroom in '68, staring in the mirror, making the identical promise to go on. Having come full circle, the ride continues. I still count my blessings very often, especially now, with the newfound blessing of having Mang Lang Orphanage and the wonderful children of Vietnam back in my life. It's much more than just gravy here on *The Other Side of War*!

I got a call in the mid '80s from the DAV (Disabled American Veterans). I had been a member since 1967 when I came home and was awarded 10 percent disability for jungle rot in my feet. The guy from DAV said, "We see in your service records that you served in areas where dioxin, Agent Orange, was sprayed and want you to know that we just got a big settlement from Dow Chemical. We want to send you the form, so that you could apply for your share of the settlement."

I said, "Okay. But can I ask you a simple question?" I think it must've been '84, because the Vietnam Memorial was about two years old. I hadn't been there yet, but I said to him, "Have you been to the memorial in Washington?"

"Yes, I have," he said.

"Well, do me a favor, the next time you go over there, take any name off the wall and send his or her mother my money, because my mother got her son back. When I went to serve the country, I didn't go to serve the country to sue. And as far as your parades go, I got my parade being born an American—that was my parade! I was supposed to serve. I owed the country. The country didn't owe me. I owed them, and if Agent Orange was part of war, it was a part of war and I accept it. I accept the responsibility for it and I'm not going to take money, knowing my mother was spared. So you give it to a mother that wasn't spared," and I hung up.

It took decades to realize I did earn it. Not until I began getting seriously ill and needed help did I become comfortable with compensation. Up to that point, I didn't feel worthy of it, and I felt like it was a slap in the face of those whose lives were taken. Fortunately, the VA has been great since my service-connected disabilities have intensified the last several years. My wife deserves a lot of credit, as well. Since she retired, we're very health conscious with foods and supplements, and I'm bouncing back well, knock on wood. It kind of put everything in perspective. I've come to terms with a lot of stuff. I found the orphanage, which allows me to deal with Vietnam because I now have a tangible positive. The other stuff will never go away.

Epilogue: Coming Out the Other Side

GOING INTO 1989, AFTER TWO YEARS ON THE ROAD AND over two hundred nights each, I began to hit my stride. I was beginning to get more and more offers from the comedy clubs to work in the third position, the closing spot, and therefore make more money. That year, I worked 212 nights from Ontario to the Cayman Islands.

I didn't get to see my parents very much at all, let alone anyone else back home. Finally, I took a short break in July before a three-week run of clubs in Canada. When I got home, I saw that my father wasn't doing well, so I insisted he see the doctor. His heart wasn't strong, and he refused to take a stress test. I was worried about his decision, but he was set in his ways and didn't need added stress.

It was also determined that his bottom teeth were horrible and putting poison in his system. I insisted we see the dentist that had helped me in 1970. I arranged to pay the bill for extracting the teeth and putting in a full denture. It felt so good to be able to provide for him, regardless of how he neglected my teeth as a child. I guess once again, I felt his pain.

Adding to the drama were my brothers. They were both divorced, with children, and constantly complaining to Mom and Dad and using them as sounding boards. I saw my mother get so red in the face and my father popping nitro pills. So before I left for Canada, I went to see both of my brothers individually and told them the exact same thing: "If you guys don't stop dumping all your problems on our parents night after night, we'll be going to the cemetery before you know it!"

I played the three weeks in Ontario, and on August 15 I arrived at Newark Airport around 11:00 a.m. The first thing I did was call my mother to let her know I was home. I told her that I would be going to the office in New York and then come home to my condo to get a good night's sleep, and that I would come to visit the following afternoon. She sounded fine. I finally got home that night around 7:00 p.m., dropped my bags, poured a scotch and water, sat down and put my head back smiling, and thought to myself, *It looks like all the hard work the last few years is paying off.*

I don't think I was on the couch more than ten minutes when the phone rang. I picked it up and couldn't believe what I heard. My mother had died in her sleep around two o'clock earlier that afternoon. I got in the car and drove down to find my father a complete wreck. He looked terrible. On top of everything else, I found out that they had let their life insurance lapse. I couldn't believe it. All they had to do is let me know and I would have paid the bills.

It was a nightmare getting the cemetery to cooperate. We had to pay for the plot for my mother and bought the one next to her for when my father would pass. They agreed to let us pay for it in installments.

My mother was so well liked; she worked at Jersey Shore Medical Center ever since my father had the heart attack in 1967. Tons of people showed up to pay their respects. Every wall was lined with flowers. It was so painful to see my father so defeated. At that point, I realized, God, he really loved my mother unconditionally. After all the infidelity and major blowouts, he was at the coffin asking her to wait for him. At that moment, I felt my entire life was put in perspective.

I did a lot of soul searching prior to the burial. After the service, I waited until everyone had left and I told the funeral director that I needed a few quiet moments with my mother. I insisted on closing the casket myself. I put my letter to her in her hands. It read, "I know you always loved me and never meant to hurt me and I forgive you! Please take this letter as a tangible symbol containing a promise that I will never raise my voice in anger or be verbally abusive to any woman for the rest of my life." And I never have till this day!

Within a few days, my father had to be put in the hospital with his heart rhythm all over the place. They finally stabilized him and allowed him to come home. I stayed up with him the rest of the week, talking until very late at night. We talked a lot about our upbringing and why he couldn't seem to get it together. He explained that after having to give up entertaining, his heart was never in anything else he did. He was tormented the rest of his life dreaming of being back on stage. I just let him talk. I saw no point in calling him out. But, I did think to myself at that moment, *God, you had five children suffering throughout our youth, how could your heart not be with us?* I let it go. I still felt his pain.

Dad seemed to be doing well enough by the weekend, so I asked my brother Richie to stay with him Saturday night so I could play a date in Waterbury, Connecticut, and return Sunday morning. I thought it would do me good, which it did. I got back to my father by noon on Sunday and even took him to a barbeque I was invited to, thinking it would do him good. Shortly after we arrived, my friend's mother took me aside and told me my father wasn't doing well and maybe I should take him home. I did. It was Sunday, September 3. That night, he ran a fever and his heart was jumping out of rhythm. I called the doctor and the jerk said to just give him Tylenol. I didn't sleep at all and then around 4:00 a.m., I heard him call to me, "Bill, please come here."

I knew then he was in very serious condition. I held his hand and said, "Dad, we better go." He agreed, and I called 911.

A policeman showed up first with oxygen and I was holding my father's hand like he was *my* son. Once again, as sad as it was, I felt blessed with another opportunity to step up to the plate for him. A few minutes before EMS arrived, his eyes went up in his head; he began to shake and held my hand so tight as he fell in my arms. At that moment, we came full circle as father and son, finding peace and closure together. *No more pain.* It was the saddest relief I'd experienced since saluting Lieutenant Klempner on my way out of Vietnam.

Interestingly, a few years later, I was playing a few dates on the west coast of Florida and visited my Aunt Ester, my father's youngest sister. We had coffee and looked at photo albums and spoke about the family. She showed me a photo of my father in his army uniform while visiting relatives in Burbank, California. Aunt Ester went on to say that after my father was discharged for medical reasons, he went to Hollywood with a friend, Vic Earlson, who was discharged the same day.

Earlson was a comedian that started in vaudeville and knew many of the stars of the day. Then my aunt dropped the bomb on me. She said after my father got home, for the next two weeks all he talked about was staying at Martha Raye's house in Bel Air his first night out of the army. Unbelievable. I wish I had known that when I was at the 8th Field Hospital and she was nursing me back from near death.

After returning from Vietnam and finally readjusting to life and my career again, the years just flew by. I often thought about my friends John Scheer and Jordan Klempner and the kids at the orphanage, but I always seemed to be distracted from finding them. But with the advent of the internet, it all seemed to fall into place more than three decades after we had said our goodbyes. Below, John and Jordan explain how we reunited, which also led to our 2013 trip back to Vietnam.

John Scheer:
"My first impressions of Billy were that he was a very bright and friendly young man and very talented musically. But we completely lost touch after Vietnam until about 2003, when I asked a mutual friend, Saul Brody, if he knew anything of Billy's whereabouts. I had been trying unsuccessfully to locate Billy for several years at that point.

"Saul came through with either an email address or a phone number. I contacted Billy, and he agreed to meet me, so I drove up to a diner near his house. Within minutes of meeting each other, the years melted away and I have felt close to him ever since."

Jordan Klempner:
"The story I have with Billy is the best friendship story I will ever have and one that brought a lot of meaning to Vietnam. I got to Vietnam in early '67. The first person I met was the mail guy, Billy Torsiello (now Terrell). We started talking every day—we just clicked. He said he was an entertainer and played guitar. I told him I played a little myself. At that time, I was very depressed about Vietnam and was looking for anything to put a smile on my face. So we started playing every night we could. We used bunkers, the mess tent, any place we could find. It was the only thing that made time pass with a smile. We even wrote our own tunes.

"Then it happened. Billy's tour was over. I was really upset about it and at the same time happy my friend was going home. I drove him to the air base. We saluted each other, and my good friend was gone, along with the best music experience I've ever had.

"Six months later I went home, started school, made new friends, played in garage bands, and when I picked up a guitar, I wondered what ever happened to Billy. Now it's 2000, the internet is here, and you can use it to find people. I knew he was from New Jersey and I got a list of phone numbers to call. In the back of my mind, I always had one thought. What if I contact him and he says, 'Jordan who?' and doesn't even remember me, because it's been over thirty-two years? So one night I'm calling, a man answers, and I say I'm looking for my friend Billy from Vietnam. The next words out of his mouth were, 'Is this Lt. Jordan Klempner?'

"Well, we both were all choked up. I yelled to my wife, 'I found him!' I told him I hoped he remembered me. And he said I was his saving grace his last four months in Vietnam. We could barely talk. I told him, if it wasn't for you I don't know how I would have gotten through Vietnam. Thirty-two years had passed, and yet it was like only one day had passed.

"He had been coming to Los Angeles for the past eighteen years to the same community where I own and operate a restaurant, to see Frankie Avalon. We soon had a reunion. I brought him to my house and I played him a song we wrote. Billy said, 'Let's write one more verse since it's only been thirty-two years.' My wife then captured it on video, and it just felt like no time has passed. Billy has remained one of my closest friends. When he told me that the orphanage was still going, he was so excited. We started talking about how the thousands of American soldiers there did many, many good things in Vietnam. And that's how we came up with the term *The Other Side of War*. There is nothing that could change our bond."

I also don't think I could have gotten through my time in Vietnam without those two guys, and I'm ever so grateful to have them back in my life.

To bring you up to date, recently I was awarded the New Jersey Vietnam Service Medal and the Distinguished Service Medal, honored by the State of New Jersey with a lot of other vets, and appreciated the citations from the governor honoring my distinguished service and my patriotism. I did a lecture at the New Jersey Vietnam Memorial and I spoke at an educational forum.

I'm still going to keep my hand in music. I've got a publishing catalog, but my focus now, going forward, is going to be getting the story out for the generations and for today's vets, about how, with time and focus, you can latch on to whatever good was there. Whether it's in Iraq with southern Iraq, the wonderful things they did with the schools or helping some of these villagers in these other areas, like we did with the children, is the good to hold on to. I have the orphanage and I have my comrades and I have PBS. So, to come full circle, at my age, I'm extremely blessed to have it in perspective.

———————

The following is a song I co-wrote with Ray Dahrouge. It expresses some of the feelings many Vietnam veterans share. Please enjoy it via YouTube.

"Gone But Not Forgotten"
(Billy Terrell and Ray Dahrouge)

With your name forever on the wall
Now at least we all have a place to go
We can pray and pay respects with them
The loved ones and the friends
We've all come to know

There's been so many questions left unanswered since my youth
I wonder if we'll ever know the truth

CHORUS:

Torn between holding on and letting go
It's got to be the hardest thing to do
Mom and I have cried our tears
We've been searching all these years for you . . . if we only knew

So much doubt we live with every day
Such a heavy price to pay
Somehow, we endure
We accept all the pain we feel
From a wound that never heals
Until we know for sure

Gone but not forgotten no matter where you are
Time won't ever take you from our hearts

REPEAT CHORUS

May the lost crew of Dustoff 90 forever rest in peace.
—Billy T.

Billy Terrell Discography

1965-2017

1965 They Said It Couldn't Be Done/The Duprees on Columbia Records (*Writer)*

1965 Never Again/The Shangri-Las on Red Bird Records (*Background Vocals*)

1968 Something Happened To Me/Central Nervous System on Laurie Records (*Writer*)

1968 Everything Is Mickey Mouse/Cartoon Candy Carnival on Metromedia Records (*Artist/Writer*)

1969 Never Gonna Let Him Know/Debbie Taylor on GWP Records (*Writer)*

1969 Baby Now There's Two of You/Terrell and Dahrouge on Metromedia Records (*Artist)*

1969 Warm Weather Music/The Three Degrees on Metromedia Records (*Writer)*

1969 Candy In The Morning/Ivory Junction on Intrepid Records (*Writer/Producer*)

1970 Where There Is Love/Anthem on Roulette Records (*Producer*)

1970 Name It And Claim It/Darryl Stewart on Wand Records (*Writer/ Producer*)

1970 Are You Really Happy/Timothy Wilson on Blue Rock Records (*Writer*)

1970 You Got To Me Stephanie/Terrell and Dahrouge on Paramount Records (*Artist/Producer*)

1970 He Knows My Key Is Always In The Mailbox/Vivian Copeland on D'Oro Records (*Writer*)

1970 Give Him Up/The Manhattans on Deluxe Records (*Writer*)

1970 A Smart Monkey Doesn't Monkey With Another Monkey's Monkey/Darryl Stewart on Musicor Records (*Producer*)

1970 You Must Know Magic/Darryl Stewart on Musicor Records (*Writer/Producer*)

1970 The Man, The Wife and The Little Baby Daughter/Phil Flowers on Bell Records (*Writer*)

1970 Don't Nobody Mess With My Baby/Debbie Taylor on Grapevine Records *(Writer/Producer)*

1970 Detour/The Persians on Grapevine Records (*Writer/Producer*)

1971 I Really Touched You Once Upon A Time/Terrell and Dahrouge on Paramount Records (*Artist/Producer*)

1971 Thursday Morning/The Last Word on Laurie Records (*Producer*)

1972 We Ain't As Tight As We Used To Be/Fredde Lowe on Polydor Records (*Writer*)

1972 Sweet Sounds Of Music/Robert John Ballack on Roulette Records (*Writer*)

1972 Givin' Up On Givin' You Up/Robert John Ballack on Roulette Records (*Writer*)

1972 I'm Slowly Losing My Mind/Fredde Lowe on Polydor Records (*Writer*)

1972 Give Him Up/The Whatnauts on GSF Records (*Writer*)

1972 Let Your Heart Be The Judge/God's Gift To Women on All Platinum Records (*Writer*)

1973 Gotta Find A Way/The Moments on Stang Records (*Writer*)

1973 He Knows My Key Will Always Be In The Mailbox/Barbara Jean English on Alithia Records (*Writer*)

1974 Mama's Side of The Bed/Benny Troy on Mercury Records (*Producer*)

1974 Key In The Mailbox/Susan Phillips on All Platinum Records (*Writer*)

1975 I've Always Had You/Benny Troy on De-Lite Records (*Writer/Producer*)

1975 The Calm Before The Storm/Benny Troy on De-Lite Records (*Writer/Producer*)

1975 Love Foundation/Electrified Action on De-Lite Records (*Writer*)

1975 I Wanna Give You Tomorrow/Benny Troy on De-Lite Records (*Writer/Producer*)

1975 I Just Don't Know How To Thank You/June Carey on De-Lite Records (*Writer/Producer*)

1975 We Ain't As Tight As We Used To Be/June Carey on De-Lite Records (*Writer/Producer*)

1976 Venus (Disco Remake)/Frankie Avalon on De-Lite Records (*Producer*)

1976 Soul On Your Side/The Rhythm Makers on Vigor Records (*Writer/Producer*)

1976 Zone/The Rhythm Makers on Vigor Records (*Producer*)

1976 I'm Gonna Love You All Over/Benny Troy on De-Lite Records (*Writer/Producer*)

1976 It's Never Too Late/Frankie Avalon on De-Lite Records (*Producer*)

1976 Gotta Get Back With You/Street People on Vigor Records (*Writer*)

1977 You're My Life/Frankie Avalon on De-Lite Records (*Producer*)

1977 Roses Grow Beyond The Wall/Frankie Avalon on De-Lite Records (*Writer/Producer*)

1977 Ecstasy, Passion and Pain/Benny Troy on De-Lite Records (*Writer/Producer*)

1977 But Not Afraid To Dream/Jimmy Druiett on Midsong Records (*Producer*)

1977 Rio De Janeiro/Gary Criss on Salsoul Records (*Writer/Producer*)

1977 Til (Disco Remake)/The Angels on Amazon Records (*Producer*)

1977 Love's Illusion/The Angels on Amazon Records (*Producer*)

1977 Rock-X-Ing/The Other Side on De-Lite Records (*Writer/Producer*)

1978 Sweet City Rhythm/Fantasia featuring Peggy Santiglia on TK Records (*Writer/Producer*)

1978 Fantasia/Carnival (Medley)/Fantasia featuring Peggy Santiglia on TK Records (*Writer/Producer*)

1978 The Calm Before The Storm/Gary Criss on Salsoul Records (*Writer/Producer*)

1978 Rio De Janeiro/The Ipanema Brothers on Barclay Records (*Writer*)

1978 Midnight Lady/Frankie Avalon on De-Lite Records (*Writer/ Producer*)

1979 Steppin' Out/Ray Dahrouge on Polydor Records (*Producer*)

1979 Dancin' Wheels/The Terrell Company on Fantasy Records (*Artist/ Writer/Producer*)

1979 Out On Fire Island/The Terrell Company on Fantasy Records (*Artist/Writer/Producer*)

1981 Fly With The Eagles/The Sharks (Philadelphia Eagles/WMMR-FM) (*Producer*)

1981 Like A Thief In The Night/Night Bandit on Cherry Hill Records (*Writer/Producer*)

1981 Mon Amour (Finally Love Has Come)/Gary Criss on Unidisc Records (*Writer/Producer*)

1983 You're The Miracle/Frankie Avalon on Bobcat Records (*Writer/ Producer*)

1983 My Boyfriend's Back (Remake)/The Angels on Tracks of My Years (Compilation released in 2010) (*Producer*)

1983 Nothin' But Heartaches/Nowhere To Run/Deborah Washington on Street Level Records (*Producer*)

1984 Hot City Nights/David Clayton Thomas on Street King Records (*Writer/Producer*)

1984 No More Writing On The Wall/LaVance on Street King Records (*Writer/Producer*)

1984 Trance Dance/Betty LaVette on Street King Records (*Dance Remix*)

1984 You Are The One/Human Nature on Street King Records (*Writer/Producer*)

1984 (The Forecast For My Life) Changed To Rain/Deborah Washington on Amazon Records (*Writer/Producer*)

1984 Innocent/Frankie Avalon on Memo Records (*Writer/Producer*)

1984 Love Exercise/Athletique on Memo Records (*Writer/Producer*)

1984 City Girl/Diane Renay (Licensed and released in 2012) (*Producer/ Remix*)

1984 Love Is Only Skin Deep/LeJeune on Artist International Records (*Writer/Producer*)

1985 Limelight/Jessica Williams on Ducal Records (*Writer/Producer*)

1985 Mysterious Kind/Jessica Williams and Helen Reddy on Ducal Records (*Producer*)

1985 Just West Of The East Side/Michael Pedicin Jr. on Billy/Gene Records (*Writer/Producer*)

1985 Love Magazine/Sylvan on Billy/Gene Records (*Writer/Producer*)

1985 Let Me Be Your Fantasy/Donna Garraffa on Artist International Records (*Dance Remix*)

1987 The Big Throwdown/Levert on Atlantic Records (*Arranger*)

1987 Sweet Sensation/Levert on Atlantic Records (*Arranger*)

1987 City Song/Michael Pedicin Jr. on Optimism Records (*Producer*)

1988 That's What Love Is/Gerald Levert and Mikki Howard on Atlantic Records (*Arranger*)

1988 Are You Ever Gonna Stop The Rain/George Kerr on Harbor Light Records (*Writer*)

1991 Especially For You/Frankie Avalon on EMI Special Markets (*Producer*)

1991 Rock & Roll Hall of Fame (New Recordings of Old Favories)/ Frankie Avalon on CEMA Special Markets (*Producer*)

1994 Because Of Love/Michael Pedicin Jr. on Passion Jazz Records (*Producer*)

1995 Reggae Christmas/Riddem Nation on Eclipse Records (*Producer*)

1996 Life of The Party (Compilation) on Q Records/QVC (*Producer*)

1996 Hooked On Disco (Compilation/Medley) on K-Tel Records (*Producer*)

1997 A Host Of Holiday Songs/QVC Hosts on Q Records (*Producer*)

1997 Phantom Phantasy/Demetrios on Naxos Jazz Records (*Producer*)

1997 Musica Caliente/Edgardo Cintron and Tiempo Noventa on Naxos Jazz Records (*Producer*)

1997 Les Mis Jazz/Demetrios on Naxos Jazz Records (*Producer*)

1997 Midnight At The Oasis (remake)/Maria Muldaur on Simitar Entainment (*Producer*)

1998 Life Of The Party 2 (Compilation) on Q Records/QVC (*Producer*)

1998 The Golden Age Of New Orleans Jazz/Louisiana Repertory Jazz Ensemble on Naxos Jazz Records (*Producer*)

1998 Moods Of Old New Orleans/Louisiana Repertory Ensemble on Naxos Jazz Records (*Producer*)

1998 Full Of Wonder/Philadelphia on Naxos Jazz Records (*Producer*)

1998 The Christmas Of Your Life/Lisa Mason on Pillow Records (*Writer/Producer*)

1999 I Am Woman/Jessica Williams/Trick Soundtrack (*Dance Remix*)

1999 When The Good Guys Used To Win/Frankie Avalon on GNP Crescendo Records (*Writer/Producer)*

1999 Frankie Avalon's Good Guys/Frankie and Friends on GNP Crescendo Records (*Producer*)

1999 New Recordings of Old Favorites/Frankie Avalon on Unidisc Records (*Producer*)

1999 Marilyn Horne Recital at Alice Tully Hall at Lincoln Center on Voices Across America (*Audio Producer*)

1999 The Best Of The Philly Sound (Compilation) on GNP Crescendo Records (*Producer*)

1999 We're At The Point Of Breakin' Up/Zabriskie Point on Hypnosis Records (*Writer*)

2000 The Best Christmas Ever/Helen Reddy on Select Media Concepts (*Writer/Producer*)

2000 Paul Sorvino Sings (PBS) on Voices Across America (*Audio Consultant*)

2000 Christmas/Helen Reddy on EMI Special Markets (*Writer/Producer*)

2001 The Very Thought Of You/Lorri Hafer & The Music of Your life Quartet on Music of Your Life (*Producer*)

2002 Merry Christmas Baby/Maria Muldaur on A Holly Jolly Christmas (*Producer*)

2002 This Christmas I Wanna Be Close To You/David Clayton Thomas on A Holly Jolly Christmas (*Producer*)

2002 Rose For My Heart/Edgardo Cintron featuring Ricky Agron on FEA Records (*Writer*)

2002 The Joy of Life/Cintron on Shark Salsa Latin Productions (*Writer*)

2002 Can't Leave Yet/Cintron on Shark Salsa Latin Productions (*Writer*)

2002 Christmas Mem'ries/Helen Reddy on BCI Eclipse Records (*Producer*)

2003 Temples of Rock/Travel Channel Documentary (*Concept Creator*)

2003 A Philadelphia Christmas/Bobby Rydell on BCI Records (*Writer/ Producer*)

2003 Something Beautiful/Bobbi Eakes on BCI Records (*Producer*)

2003 Who Are These Strangers/Michael Feinstein on BCI Records (*Producer*)

2004 An Old Fashion Christmas/Lorrie Morgan on St. Nicholas Music (*Producer*)

2005 Want You/Tony DeSare on Telarc Records (*Producer*)

2006 (I'd Have It All) If I Had Drew/Tony DeSare on My Date With Drew Soundtrack (*Producer)*

2006 Reader's Digest/Music of Your Life CD Compilation series on BCI Records via Walmart (*Concept Consultant*)

2007 Painted Mem'ries/John Gabriel on GNP Crescendo Records (*Producer*)

2007 First Last Kiss/Tony DeSare on Telarc Records (*Producer*)

2009 Radio Show/Tony DeSare on Telarc Records (*Producer*)

2010 The Strayhorn Project/Don Braden and Mark Rapp on Premium Music Solutions (*Producer*)

2010 Larry Carlton Plays The Sound of Philadelphia on 335 Records (*Producer*)

2010 Another Night In San Juan/Cintron Anthology on CAMJAM Records (*Writer*)

2016 The Applejacks on Dave Appell Music (*Production Consultant*)

2017 Never, Never Love/The Applejax featuring Larry Carlton on Dave Appell Music (*Producer*)

2017 Ridin' High/The Applejax featuring Paul Shaffer on Dave Appell Music (*Producer*)

2017 When Christmas Was Christmas/Debbie Williams on 335 Records (*Writer/Producer*)

Tribute: Here's To The Band!

I can't sign off without paying tribute to many of the people I've been blessed to know and work with all these years. Wonderfully talented musicians, arrangers, recording engineers and studios who have enriched my life and music along the way. I'm forever grateful!

Arrangers:

Artie Butler, Gary Sherman, Joe Renzetti, Tony Camillo, Richard Tee, Charlie Callelo, Richard Rome, Larry Fallon, Bert Keyes, John Davis, Pete Dino, Lee Holdrige, Ed Bland, Bert De Coteaux, Tony DeSare, Alex Rybeck, Demetrios Pappas, Evan Solot.

New York Studios:

Variety Recording, ODO Recording Studios, Musicor Records Studios, Columbia Records Studios, RCA Records Studios, The Record Plant, A&R Studios, Dick Charles Studios, Associated Recording, Sigma Sound Studios, Century Sound Studios, Allegro Studios, Mercury Records Studios, CI Recording, Regent Sound Studios, Broadway Recording Studios, The Hit Factory, Nola

Recording Studios, Media Sound, Green Street Studios, Unique Recording Studios, Excalibur Recording, Platinum Studios, 39th Street Studios, Avatar Studios, The Power Station.

New Jersey Studios:
Vantone Recording Studios, The House of Music, Giant Steps Recording Studios, Super Sound Studios.

Philadelphia Studios:
Sigma Sound Studios, Starr Recording Studios, Alpha Recording Studios, Ridge Sound Studios, 4th Street Recording Studios.

Nashville Studios:
Glaser Brothers Studios, The Bennett House, The Fun House, Out Landis Recording.

Chicago: Paragon Recording Studios.

Los Angeles: United Western Recording Studios.

Engineers:
Fred Vargas, Joe Tarsia, Jim Czak, John Post, Bill Moss, Andy Abrams, Michael Hutchinson, Gene Leone, Ken Present, Bob May, Gene Radice, Bill Radice, Al Vanderbilt, Pat Jacques, Michael Tarsia, Bruce Staple, Tony Bongiovi, Mark Snow, Gene Eichelberger, Steve Jerome, Chuck Britz, Gary Kellgren, Terry Rosiello, Bruce Tergesen, Jerry Ragavoy, Vic Stevens, Brooks Arthur, Roy Cicala, Barry Mraz, Chuck Irvin, Vince Oddo, Artie Polhemus, Eddie Ciletti, Jim Salamone, and Goedfrey Diamond.

Piano/Organ/Keyboards:

Frank Owens, Paul Griffin, Ben Lanzaroni, Richard Tee, Paul Shaffer, Leon Pindarvis, Richard Rome, Demetrios Pappas, Cotton Kent, John Davis, Billy Biddle, Tony DeSare, Alex Rybeck, Frank Strauss, Shane Keister.

Bass:

Chuck Rainey, Bob Babbitt, Will Lee, Andy Lasasis, Gerald Veasley, Steve Beskrone, Christopher Li'nard Jackson, Vince Fay, Chico Huff, Mike Lee, John Arbo, Alan Gorrie.

Drums:

Bobby Gregg, Gary Chester, Herbie Lovell, Jimmy Johnson, Jimmy Young, Alan Schwartzberg, Bernard Purdie, Vic Stevens, Grant MacAvoy, Andrea Valentini, Jerry Carrigan.

Guitar:

Larry Carlton, Rick Derringer, Hugh McCracken, Jeff Miranov, Bob Rose, Onnie McIntire, Cornell Dupree, Carl Lynch, TJ Tindall, Craig Snyder, Tommy Byrnes, Bucky Pizzarelli, Dave Gellis, Pete Bordanelli, Alan Slutsky, Danny Eyer, Mario Infanti.

Percussion:

Jimmy Maelen, Carlos Martin, Larry Washington, Nick D'Amico, Hector Rosado, Edgardo Cintron.

Brass & Reeds:

Ron Kerber, Artie Kaplan, George Young, Mark Douthit, Michael Pedicin, Jr, Chris Farr, Carl Cox, Bob Ferguson, Clint Sharman, John Swana, Don Braden, Mark Rapp, Steve Guttman, Nick Marchione, Dale Kirkland, Chris Komer, Alan Rubin, and Clark Terry.

Background vocals:

Linda November, Vivian Reed, Gwen Guthrie, Toni Wine, Carla Benson, Charlene Holloway, Vaneese Thomas, Carolyn Mitchell

I must also pay tribute to the late Don Renaldo and the MFSB Orchestra in Philadelphia and the late Irving Spice and his string section in New York back in the good old days.

I would like to extend a very special thanks to Jon Singer, Art Levy, and the wonderful staff at Spirit Music Group for their gracious friendship and support.

—Billy T.

Been There . . . Still There!